# Poems for Kids

Over 600 poems for teaching
poetry terms & poetic devices
to children in grades 3-6

Selected by

Lorrie L. Birchall

for James,

my first grandchild

Poems for Kids: Over 600 poems for teaching poetry terms & poetic devices
to children in grades 3-6

Copyright ©2021 by Lorrie L. Birchall
All Rights Reserved.

ISBN: 9798513641742

Cover illustrations by Katerina Davidenko at Bubert Art

# Table of Contents

# Introduction

## Hello Teachers!

If you're teaching students about poetry, you need poems—lots and lots of poems! I've assembled some of my very favorite poem exemplars and organized them to make it convenient for you to SHOW your students poetry terms & poetic devices in context. This HUGE poetry anthology also includes a wide variety of poet voices in different bands of complexity to help you choose poems to meet the unique and individualized needs of *your* students.

This is a very child-friendly collection of poems, but that being said, there's no reason why middle and upper elementary students can't be exposed to *some* of the "adult" poetry of Henry Wadsworth Longfellow, Emily Dickinson, Paul Laurence Dunbar, Walt Whitman, Carl Sandburg, Robert Frost, and others. Children will have a much greater appreciation and understanding of the rich vocabulary and figurative language found in poetry if they are exposed to it early and often. A deeper and more nuanced understanding of some of the poems will continue to grow over time.

The poems in this collection are generally short (or at least "shortish") to help you really target your teaching of specific poetry terms & poetic devices in a mini-lesson. Simple illustrations add additional picture support to enhance comprehension in all students, but especially English language learners.

Even if you've never taught poetry before, this organized and accessible collection of over 600 poems will make it far easier to teach your students all about poetry terms & poetic devices! I've included the Common Core State Standards related to poetry, as there are quite a few in grades 3-6.

I think you just can't have too many poems!

Lorrie L. Birchall

# Common Core State Standards Related to Poetry

# 3<sup>rd</sup> Grade Standards

**READING LITERATURE: CCSS.ELA-LITERACY.RL.3.5**

Refer to parts of stories, dramas, and poems when writing or speaking about a text, using terms such as chapter, scene, and stanza; describe how each successive part builds on earlier sections.

**LANGUAGE: CCSS.ELA-LITERACY.L.3.5**

Demonstrate understanding of figurative language, word relationships and nuances in word meanings.

**READING LITERATURE:  CCSS.ELA-LITERACY.RL.3.10**

By the end of the year, read and comprehend literature, including stories, dramas, and poetry, at the high end of the grades 2-3 text complexity band independently and proficiently.

**FLUENCY:  CCSS.ELA-LITERACY.RF.3.4.B**

Read grade-level prose and poetry orally with accuracy, appropriate rate, and expression on successive readings.

# 4th Grade Standards

**LANGUAGE:  CCSS.ELA-LITERACY.L.4.5**

Demonstrate understanding of figurative language, word relationships, and nuances in word meanings.

**FLUENCY:  CCSS.ELA-LITERACY.RF.4.4.B**

Read grade-level prose and poetry orally with accuracy, appropriate rate, and expression on successive readings

**READING LITERATURE:  CCSS.ELA-LITERACY.RL.4.5**

Explain major differences between poems, drama, and prose, and refer to the structural elements of poems (e.g., verse, rhythm, meter) and drama (e.g., casts of characters, settings, descriptions, dialogue, stage directions) when writing or speaking about a text.

**READING LITERATURE:  CCSS.ELA-LITERACY.RL.4.6**

Compare and contrast the point of view from which different stories are narrated, including the difference between first- and third-person narrations.

**READING LITERATURE:  CCSS.ELA-LITERACY.RL.4.10**

By the end of the year, read and comprehend literature, including stories, dramas, and poetry, in the grades 4-5 text complexity band proficiently, with scaffolding as needed at the high end of the range.

# 5<sup>th</sup> Grade Standards

**FLUENCY: CCSS.ELA-LITERACY.RF.5.4.B**

Read grade-level prose and poetry orally with accuracy, appropriate rate, and expression on successive readings.

**LANGUAGE: CCSS.ELA-LITERACY.L.5.5**

Demonstrate understanding of figurative language, word relationships, and nuances in word meanings.

**LANGUAGE: CCSS.ELA-LITERACY.L.5.5.A**

Interpret figurative language, including similes and metaphors, in context.

**READING LITERATURE: CCSS.ELA-LITERACY.RL.5.5**

Explain how a series of chapters, scenes, or stanzas fits together to provide the overall structure of a particular story, drama, or poem.

# 6<sup>th</sup> Grade Standards

**LANGUAGE: CCSS.ELA-LITERACY.L.6.5**

Demonstrate understanding of figurative language, word relationships, and nuances in word meanings.

**LANGUAGE: CCSS.ELA-LITERACY.L.6.5.A**

Interpret figures of speech (e.g., personification) in context.

**READING LITERATURE: CCSS.ELA-LITERACY.RL.6.10**

By the end of the year, read and comprehend literature, including stories, dramas, and poems, in the grades 6-8 text complexity band proficiently, with scaffolding as needed at the high end of the range.

# What is Alliteration?

Alliteration is the repetition of the
*same beginning* **sound** (not alphabet letter) of nearby words.
It can sometimes be a tongue twister, but it isn't always.

Alliteration **m**akes language **m**uch **m**ore **m**emorable.

The following poem, "The Swan," repeats many words that begin with the *s sound*,
so it *is* a bit of a tongue twister.

## The Swan by Unknown

**S**wan **s**wims over the **s**ea—
**S**wim, swan, swim;
**S**wan **s**wam back again,
Well **s**wam, **s**wan.

The following poem repeats several *different beginning sounds* in the poem.

## A Lazy Day by Paul Laurence Dunbar

The trees bend down along the stream,
Where anchored swings my tiny boat.
The **d**ay is one to **d**rowse and **d**ream
And list the **thr**ushes **thr**ottling note.
When music from his **b**osom **b**leeds
Among the **r**iver's **r**ustling **r**eeds.

9

# Alliteration

## The 4:04 Train by Carolyn Wells

"There's a train at 4:04," said Miss Jenny;
Four tickets I'll take. Have you any?"
Said the man at the door: "Not four for 4:04,
For four for 4:04 is too many."

## The Tutor by Carolyn Wells

A tutor who tootled the flute
Was teaching two tooters to toot.
Said the two to the tutor,
"Is it harder to toot,
Or to tutor two tooters to toot?"

## Write is Right by Unknown

"Write," we know is written right
when we see it written "write."
But when we see it written "wright,"
we know 'tis not, then, written right.
For "write," to have it written right
Must not be written "right" or "wright,"
nor yet should it be written "rite,"
but "write," for so 'tis written right.

# Alliteration

## The Spider by Lorrie L. Birchall

The spider spins her web of lace,

which sparkles in her tiny space.

She is a splendid little spy,

when she spots her prey—the fly.

## The Jellyfish by Lorrie L.Birchall

The jellyfish—

stringy,

swingy,

springy,

STINGY!

## Mr. Gruff by Lorrie L. Birchall

Mr. Gruff is such a grouch;

He likes to gripe and groan.

He grumbles when he greets you—

It's no wonder he's alone.

# Alliteration

## Babies by LeRoy F. Jackson

Come to the land where the babies grow,

Like flowers in the green, green grass.

Tiny babes that swing and crow

Whenever the warm winds pass,

And laugh at their own bright eyes aglow

In a fairy looking-glass.


Come to the sea where the babies sail

In ships of shining pearl,

Borne to the west by a golden gale

Of sun-beams all awhirl;

And perhaps a baby brother will sail

To you, my little girl.

## Christopher Crump by LeRoy F. Jackson

Christopher Crump,

All in a lump,

Sits like a toad on the top of a stump.

He stretches and sighs,

And blinks with his eyes,

Bats at the beetles and fights off the flies.

# Alliteration

## Weather by Unknown

Whether the weather be fine
Or whether the weather be not,
Whether the weather be cold,
Or whether the weather be hot,
We'll weather the weather
Whatever the weather,
Whether we like it or not.

## The Firefly by Evaleen Stein

Flash and flicker and fly away,
Trailing light as you flutter far,
Are you a lamp for the fairies, say?
Or a flake of fire from a falling star?

## A Fly and a Flea in a Flue by Unknown

A fly and a flea in a flue
Were imprisoned, so what could they do?
   Said the fly, "Let us flee!"
   "Let us fly!" said the flea,
And they flew through a flaw in the flue.

# Alliteration

## Hush-A-Bye-Baby -Traditional Nursery Rhyme

Hush-a-bye baby, on the tree-top,

When the wind blows the cradle will rock;

When the bough breaks the cradle will fall—

Down will come baby, cradle and all!

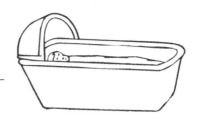

## Lucy Locket -Traditional Nursery Rhyme

Lucy Locket lost her pocket,

Kitty Fisher found it.

Not a penny was there in it,

Only ribbon round it

## Sing a Song of Sixpence -Traditional Nursery Rhyme

Sing a song of sixpence, a pocketful of rye,

Four-and-twenty blackbirds baked in a pie;

When the pie was opened the birds began to sing,

Wasn't that a dainty dish to set before the King?

# Alliteration

## The Codfish by Unknown

The codfish lays ten thousand eggs,
The homely hen lays one.
The codfish never cackles
To tell you what she's done.

And so we scorn the codfish,
While the humble hen we prize,
Which only goes to show you
That it pays to advertise.

## The Pirate's Parrot by Unknown

I am the pirate's parrot,
I sail the seven seas
And sleep inside the crow's nest
Don't look for me in trees!

I am the pirate's parrot,
A bird both brave and bold.
I guard the captain's treasure
And count his hoard of gold.

# Alliteration

## The Man in the Moon by Unknown

The man in the moon as he sails the sky

Is a very remarkable skipper.

But he made a mistake

When he tried to take

A drink of milk from the dipper.

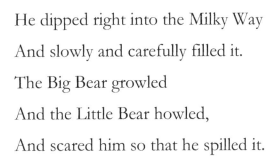

He dipped right into the Milky Way

And slowly and carefully filled it.

The Big Bear growled

And the Little Bear howled,

And scared him so that he spilled it.

## Tired Tim by Walter de la Mare

Poor Tired Tim! It's sad for him.

He lags the long bright morning through,

Ever so tired of nothing to do.

He moons and mopes the livelong day,

Nothing to think about, nothing to say.

Up to bed with his candle to creep,

Too tired to yawn, too tired to sleep.

Poor Tired Tim! It's sad for him.

# Alliteration

## I Am a Snail by Unknown

I am a Snail

And my tell-trail

Is what I leave

Behind.  Believe

Me when I say

I'm built this way—

My tummy slime

Is scummy.  I'm

A crawling mess

Of stickiness,

And in my wake,

Make no mistake,

my distur-

bing signature. - - - - - - -

## A Sailor Went to Sea by Unknown

A sailor went to sea

to see what he could see.

And all that he could see

was sea, sea, sea.

# Alliteration

## Woodland in Autumn by Unknown

No sound was in the woodlands
Save the squirrel's dropping shell
And the yellow leaves among the boughs,
Low rustling as they fell.

At last after watching and waiting,
Autumn, the beautiful came,
Stepping with sandals silver,
Decked with her mantle of flame.

## The Bumblebee by Laura E. Richards

The bumblebee, the bumblebee,
He flew to the top of the tulip-tree.
He flew to the top, but he could not stop,
For he had to get home to his early tea.

The bumblebee, the bumblebee,
He flew away from the tulip-tree;
But he made a mistake, and flew into the lake,
And he never got home to his early tea.

# Alliteration

## Lost by Carl Sandburg

Desolate and lone

All night long on the lake

Where fog trails and mist creeps,

The whistle of a boat

Calls and cries unendingly,

Like some lost child

In tears and trouble

Hunting the harbor's breast

And the harbor's eyes.

## Flux by Carl Sandburg

Sand of the sea runs red

Where the sunset reaches and quivers.

Sand of the sea runs yellow

Where the moon slants and wavers.

## From the Shore by Carl Sandburg

A lone gray bird,

Dim-dipping, far-flying,

Alone in the shadows and grandeurs and tumults,

Of night and the sea,

And the stars and storms.

# Alliteration

## The Brook by Alfred Lord Tennyson

I slip, I slide, I gloom, I glance,
Among my skimming swallows;
I make the netted sunbeam dance
Against my sandy shallows.

I murmur under moon and stars
In brambly wildernesses;
I linger by my shingly bars;
I loiter round my cresses;

And out again I curve and flow
To join the brimming river,
For men may come and men may go,
But I go on for ever.

## The Beetle by Edith King

The other day, to my surprise,
I saw a beetle blue
Spread slowly out and fly away—
I never knew he flew.

# Alliteration

## Whistle by Unknown

I want to learn to whistle,
I've always wanted to;
I fix my mouth to do it, but,
The whistle won't come through.

I think perhaps it's stuck, and so
I try it once again;
Can people swallow whistles,
Where is my whistle then?

## Whirl and Twirl by Unknown

Like a leaf or a feather,
In the windy, windy weather,
We will whirl around,
And twirl around,
And all sink down together.

# What is Allusion?

An allusion makes a brief, intentional reference to just about anything.

It could be a historical, mythic, or literary person,

place, event, expression, or movement.

To fully understand the poem, it helps to understand the reference.

Example:

The poem, "Where Bobby Lives," **alludes** (refers to) to the nursery rhyme, "Jack and Jill."

Original Nursery Rhyme:

# Jack and Jill —Traditional Nursery Rhyme

Jack and Jill went up the hill

To fetch a pail of water.

Jack fell down and broke his crown,

And Jill came tumbling after.

Allusion to the Nursery Rhyme:

# Where Bobby Lives by Peter Newell

Where Bobby lives there is a hill—

A hill so steep and high,

'Twould fill the bill for Jack and Jill

Their famous act to try.

# Allusion

Original Nursery Rhyme:

## The Old Woman Who Lived in a Shoe

There was an old woman who lived in a shoe.

She had so many children, she didn't know what to do.

She gave them some broth without any bread;

And kissed them all soundly and put them to bed.

Allusion to the Nursery Rhyme:

## Who Lived in a Shoe? by Beatrix Potter

You know that old woman

Who lived in a shoe?

She had so many children

She didn't know what to do?

I think if she lived in

A little shoe-house

That little old lady

Was surely a mouse!

# Allusion

Original Nursery Rhyme:

## Mary, Mary, Quite Contrary

Mary, Mary, quite contrary
How does your garden grow?
With silver bells and cockleshells
And pretty maids all in a row.

Allusion to the Nursery Rhyme:

## Contrary Mary by Nancy Byrd Turner

You ask why Mary was called contrary?
Well, this is why, my dear:
She planted the most outlandish things
In her garden every year;
She was always sowing the oddest seed,
And when advised to stop,
Her answer was merely, "No indeed—
Just wait till you see my crop!"

# Allusion

Original Nursery Rhyme:

## Hush-a-Bye Baby -Traditional Nursery Rhyme

Hush-a-bye baby, on the tree-top,

When the wind blows the cradle will rock;

When the bough breaks the cradle will fall—

Down will come baby, cradle and all!

Allusion to the Nursery Rhyme:

## The Mouse's Lullaby by Palmer Cox

Oh, rock-a-bye, mousie, rock-a-bye so!

When baby's asleep to the baker's I'll go,

And while he's not looking I'll pop from a hole,

And bring to my baby a fresh little roll.

# Allusion

Original Nursery Rhyme:

## Little Boy Blue

Little Boy Blue, come blow your horn,

The sheep's in the meadow, the cow's in the corn.

But where is the boy who looks after the sheep?

He's under a haystack, fast asleep.

Original Nursery Rhyme:

## Little Bo Peep

Little Bo-Peep has lost her sheep,

And can't tell where to find them;

Leave them alone, and they'll come home,

Bringing their tails behind them.

Allusion to the *two* Nursery Rhymes:

# An Intercepted Valentine by Carolyn Wells

Little Bo-Peep, will you be mine?

I want you for my Valentine.

You are my choice of all the girls,

With your blushing cheeks and your fluttering curls,

With your ribbons pink and your kirtle neat,

None other is so fair and sweet.

Little Bo-Peep, let's run away,

And marry each other on Midsummer Day;

And ever to you I'll be fond and true,

Your faithful Valentine,

Little Boy Blue

# Charlotte's Web for Wilbur by Lorrie L. Birchall

Charlotte is a spider,
who weaves her letters BIG,
to liberate young Wilbur,
who really is SOME PIG!

# Allusion

## Napoleon by Oliver Herford

I like to draw Napoleon best

Because one hand is in his vest,

The other hand behind his back.

(For drawing hands I have no knack.

## That Old Joke by W.M. Thackeray

True wit was seldom heard,

And humor shown by few,

When reigned King George the Third,

And that old joke was new.

## Medusa by Oliver Herford

How did Medusa do her hair?

The question fills me with despair.

It must have caused her sore distress

That head of curling snakes to dress.

Whenever after endless toil

She coaxed it finally to coil,

And, being woman and aware

Of such disaster to her hair,

What *could* she do but petrify

All whom she met, with freezing eye?

# Allusion

## A Modern Invention by Carolyn Wells

Old Santa Claus is up-to-date,

And hereafter, rumors say,

He'll come with his pack of glittering toys,

And visit the homes of girls and boys,

In a new reindeerless sleigh.

## C is the Crocodile by Oliver Herford

C is the crocodile creepy who ate

The right hand of Hook and covets its mate.

He makes a loud ticking wherever he goes

For he swallowed a clock (To kill time I suppose).

## The Fishes by Oliver Herford

Now forth to fish goes good Saint Valentine,

And baits his gentle hook with tender wishes,

Cupid has lent his bow for rod and line.

Alas! Our time has come—we are the fishes.

# Allusion

## The Fate of a Turkey Gobbler by Edwin C. Ranck

I'm just a turkey gobbler,

But I've got a word to say

And I'd like to say it quickly

Before I pass away,

For I will get it in the neck

Upon Thanksgiving Day.

I cannot keep from thinking

Of poor Marie Antoinette,

She lost her head completely,

But this is what I'll get—

They'll knock the stuffin' out o' me

Without the least regret.

I've just a few days left now

Before I meet my fate,

For every turkey gets the axe,

The little and the great.

There never was a turkey born

Who didn't fill a plate.

# What is Anaphora?

Anaphora is the **repetition of a word or phrase**
**at the beginning** of verses, clauses or paragraphs.

**Anaphora** is used in order to **show emphasis**.

Examples:

Notice how a **word** or **phrase** is repeated at the beginning of several poetry lines.

## Hurt No Living Thing by Christina Georgina Rossetti

Hurt no living thing:

Ladybird, nor butterfly,

**Nor** moth with dusty wing,

**Nor** cricket chirping cheerily,

**Nor** grasshopper so light of leap,

**Nor** dancing gnat, nor beetle fat,

**Nor** harmless worms that creep.

## Mother's Song by Unknown

**Ten thousand** parks where deer do run,

**Ten thousand** roses in the sun,

**Ten thousand** pearls beneath the sea,

My babe more precious is to me.

# Anaphora

Some nursery rhymes use anaphora.

## This Little Piggie -Traditional Nursery Rhyme

This little piggy went to market,

This little piggy stayed home,

This little piggy had roast beef,

This little piggy had none.

This little piggy cried ... wee, wee, wee,

all the way home!

## The House That Jack Built -Traditional Nursery Rhyme

This is the farmer sowing the corn,

That kept the cock that crowed in the morn,

That waked the priest all shaven and shorn,

That married the man all tattered and torn,

That kissed the maiden all forlorn,

That milked the cow with the crumpled horn,

That tossed the dog,

That worried the cat,

That killed the rat,

That ate the malt

That lay in the house that Jack built.

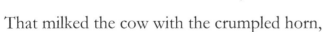

# Anaphora

## A Farm Story -Traditional Nursery Rhyme

The cock's on the housetop blowing his horn;
The bull's in the barn a-threshing of corn;
The maids in the meadows are making of hay;
The ducks in the river are swimming away.

## For Baby -Traditional Nursery Rhyme

You shall have an apple,
You shall have a plum,
You shall have a rattle,
When papa comes home.

## Sneezing -Traditional Nursery Rhyme

If you sneeze on Monday, you sneeze for danger;
Sneeze on a Tuesday, kiss a stranger;
Sneeze on a Wednesday, sneeze for a letter;
Sneeze on a Thursday, something better.
Sneeze on a Friday, sneeze for sorrow;
Sneeze on a Saturday, joy tomorrow.

# Anaphora

## The Little Turtle by Vachel Lindsay

There was a little turtle.

He lived in a box.

He swam in a puddle.

He climbed on the rocks.

He snapped at a mosquito.

He snapped at a flea.

He snapped at a minnow.

And he snapped at me.

He caught the mosquito.

He caught the flea.

He caught the minnow.

But he didn't catch me.

## Little Wind by Unknown

Little wind, blow on the hilltop;

Little wind, blow on the plain,

Little wind, blow up the sunshine,

Little wind, blow off the rain.

# Anaphora

## Only One Mother by George Cooper

Hundreds of stars in the pretty sky,
Hundreds of shells on the shore together,
Hundreds of birds that go singing by,
Hundreds of lambs in the sunny weather.

Hundreds of dewdrops to greet the dawn,
Hundreds of bees in the purple clover,
Hundreds of butterflies on the lawn,
But only one mother the wide world over.

## Our Puppies by Evaleen Stein

Little ears as soft as silk,
Little teeth as white as milk,
Little noses cool and pink,
Little eyes that blink and blink,
Little bodies round and fat,
Little hearts that pit-a-pat,
Surely prettier puppies never
Were before nor can be ever!

# Anaphora

## Kind Hearts by Henry Wadsworth Longfellow

Kind hearts are the gardens,
Kind thoughts are the roots,
Kind words are the blossoms,
Kind deeds are the fruits;

Love is the sweet sunshine
That warms into life,
For only in darkness
Grow hatred and strife.

## Skyscrapers by Rachel Field

Do skyscrapers ever grow tired
    Of holding themselves up high?
Do they ever shiver on frosty nights
    With their tops against the sky?
Do they feel lonely sometimes,
    Because they have grown so tall?
Do they ever wish they could just lie down
    And never get up at all?

# Anaphora

## Kite Weather by Ralph Bergengren

To the South the geese are going.

Across the world a breeze is blowing—

Blowing leaves from every tree,

Blowing ships upon the sea,

Blowing hats off people's heads,

Blowing chimney smoke to threads,

Blowing till the curtain flutters,

Slamming doors, and shaking shutters.

Then's the time to fly your kite,

But you have to hold it tight!

## Forget by M.M. Dryden

Forget the slander you have heard,

Forget the hasty unkind word,

Forget the quarrel and the cause,

Forget the whole affair because

Forget it is the only way—

Forget the storm of yesterday.

# Anaphora

## What Do We Plant? by Henry Abbey

What do we plant when we plant the tree?

We plant the ship, which will cross the sea.

We plant the mast to carry the sails;

We plant the planks to withstand the gales—

The keel, the keelson, and the beam and knee;

We plant the ship when we plant the tree.

What do we plant when we plant the tree?

We plant the houses for you and me.

We plant the rafters, the shingles, the floors.

We plant the studding, the lath, the doors,

The beams, and siding, all parts that be;

We plant the house when we plant the tree.

What do we plant when we plant the tree?

A thousand things that we daily see;

We plant the spire that out-towers the crag,

We plant the staff for our country's flag,

We plant the shade, from the hot sun free;

We plant all these when we plant the tree.

# Anaphora

## The Pessimist by Benjamin Franklin King

Nothing to do but work,
Nothing to eat but food,
Nothing to wear but clothes
To keep one from going nude.

Nothing to breathe but air
Quick as a flash it's gone;
Nowhere to fall but off,
Nowhere to stand but on.

Nothing to comb but hair,
Nowhere to sleep but in bed,
Nothing to weep but tears,
Nothing to bury but dead.

Nothing to sing but songs,
Ah, well, alas! Alack!
Nowhere to go but out,
Nowhere to come but back.

Nothing to see but sights,
Nothing to quench but thirst,
Nothing to have but what we've got;
Thus through life we are cursed.

Nothing to strike but a gait;
Everything moves that goes.
Nothing at all but common sense
Can ever withstand these woes.

# What is Anthropomorphism?

(pronounced an-thruh-puh-**mor**-fizm)

Anthropomorphism is a type of personification.

Personification gives human characteristics to animals, objects,

or concepts to create imagery.

Anthropomorphism tries to make an animal, object, or concept behave

and appear as if it *is* a human being.

Use of dialogue is a BIG clue.

If a non-human is talking,

it's an anthropomorphic character.

Example of a **personified** (humanized) teapot:

The teapot whistled and hissed impatiently.

Example of **anthropomorphized** teapot:

"I'm boiling already!" exclaimed the teapot loudly.

Example of a **personified** (humanized) wolf:

The devious wolf loitered leisurely around the forest all day.

Example of an **anthropomorphized** wolf:

"Little Pig, Little Pig, let me come in, or I'll blow your house down!" shouted the Big Bad Wolf.

# Anthropomorphism

## Come, Little Leaves by George Cooper

"Come, little leaves," said the wind one day,

"Come o'er the meadows with me and play;

Put on your dresses of red and gold,

For summer is gone and the days grow cold."

Soon as the leaves heard the wind's loud call,

Down they came fluttering, one and all;

Over the brown fields they danced and flew,

singing the glad little songs they knew.


"Cricket, goodbye, we've been friends so long;

Little brook, sing us your farewell song;

Say you are sorry to see us go;

Ah, you will miss us, right well we know."


"Dear little lambs in your fleecy fold,

Mother will keep you from harm and cold;

fondly we watched you in vale and glade;

Say, will you dream of our loving shade?"


Dancing and whirling, the little leaves went;

Winter had called them, and they were content;

soon, fast asleep in their earthy beds,

The snow laid a coverlid over their heads.

41

# Anthropomorphism

## The Icicle by A.S.C.

An icicle hung on a red brick wall,

And it said to the sun, "I don't like you at all!"

—drip, drip, drip.


But the sun said, "Dear, you've a saucy tongue,

And you should remember, I'm old and you're young."

—drip, drip, drip.


But the icicle only cried the more,

Though the good sun smiled on it just as before,

Until at the end of the winter day,

It had cried its poor little self away!

—drip, drip, drip.


## What the Worm Wants by LeRoy F. Jackson

"Oh," said the worm,

"I'm awfully tired of sitting in the trees;

I want to be a butterfly

And chase the bumblebees."

# What is Assonance?

Assonance is the repetition of the same
**vowel sounds** in nearby words.
(Helpful Hint: Have a partner read the poem aloud
and just *listen* for inner vowel <u>sounds</u> in the words.)


Assonance makes language more engaging to the ear.
The vowels are:  a  e  i  o  u


Examples:  That man has a travel bag. (Repetition of short ă sound)

Jill Higgins will pick a finish for the big kitchen. (short ĭ sound)


## The Crocus by Walter Crane

The golden crocus reaches up          (long ō sound)
To catch a sunbeam in her cup.        (short ŭ sound)


## Night by William Blake

The moon, like a flower
In heaven's high bower,
With **silent delight,**          (long ī sound)
Sits and **smiles** on the **night**.      (long ī sound)

# Assonance

## Moses by Unknown

Moses supposes his toeses are roses,
But Moses supposes erroneously;
For nobody's toeses are posies of roses
As Moses supposes his toeses to be.

## Nightlights by Unknown

There is no need to light a nightlight
On a light night like tonight;
For a nightlight's light's a slight light
When the moonlight's white and bright.

## King and Queen of the Pelicans by Edward Lear

King and Queen of the Pelicans we;
No other Birds so grand we see!
None but we have feet like fins!
With lovely leathery throats and chins!
Ploffskin, Pluffskin, Pelican jee!
We think no Birds so happy as we!
Plumpskin, Ploshkin, Pelican Jill!
We think so then, and we thought so still.

44

# Assonance

## Otter and Frog by Lorrie L. Birchall

Otter got on top a rock
to see his friend the frog.
The rock was hot, so they hopped off—
and swam across the bog.

## Mice in Line by Lorrie L. Birchall

A wise old cat shined up a slide—
and five white mice lined up to ride.
The wise old cat had seemed so nice—
until he dined on five white mice.

## The Spider's Web by Lorrie L. Birchall

The spider spins her sticky web
and never will deny,
she patiently is waiting for
some bugs to mummify.

# Assonance

## Alas, Alack! by Walter de la Mare

Ann, Ann! Come quick as you can!

There's a fish that talks in the frying-pan.

Out of the fat, as clear as glass,

He put up his mouth and moaned 'Alas!'

Oh, most mournful, 'Alas, alack!'

Then turned to his sizzling, and sank him back.

## Old Hogan's Goat by Unknown

Old Hogan's goat was feeling fine,

Ate six red shirts from off the line;

Old Hogan grabbed him by the back

And tied him to the railroad track.

Now when the train came into sight,

That goat grew pale and green with fright;

He heaved a sigh, as if in pain,

Coughed up those shirts and flagged the train!

# Assonance

## I Saw Essau by Unknown

I saw Essau sawing wood,

And Essau saw I saw him;

Though Essau saw I saw him saw,

Still Essau went on sawing.

## Tommy Trimble by LeRoy F. Jackson

Billy be nimble,

Hurry and see

Old Tommy Trimble

Climbing a tree.

He claws with his fingers

And digs with his toes.

The longer he lingers

The slower he goes

# What is Consonance?

Consonance is the repetition of the same
(primarily inner and ending) **consonant *sounds***
of nearby words.

Consonance brings attention to the many
consonant sounds in language.

Remember: If a letter isn't a vowel (a, e, i, o, u), it's a consonant.

Examples:

I dropped my so**ck** in thi**ck**, sti**ck**y mud.          (k sound)

We**n**dy ca**n** se**n**d Ke**nn**y gree**n** bea**n**s.          (n sound)

Cli**ff**ord the ele**ph**ant has an awful tele**ph**one.          (f sound…not letter)

## Kings Live in Palaces by Hilaire Belloc

Kings live in Palaces, and Pigs in sties,          (z sound)

And youth in Expectation. Youth is wise.          (n sound & z sound)

## Mr. Pelican by Elizabeth Gordan

Here is old Mr. Pelican,

He is a famous fisherman;

Said he: "I do not mind wet feet

If I catch fish enough to eat."

# Consonance

## Jelly on the Plate by Unknown

Jelly on the plate,

Jelly on the plate.

Wibble, wobble,

Wibble, wobble,

Jelly on the plate.

### Iddy Biddy by Unknown

Iddy Biddy was a mouse,

Iddy Biddy had no spouse.

Iddy Biddy wasn't pretty,

Oh, by gosh, it was a pity.

## Arthur and His Father by Unknown

Arthur and his father,

They rode from south to north,

The length and breadth of England,

To reach the Firth of Forth.

Then they raced each other northwards,

For all that they were worth,

And father reached Midlothian

As Arthur stopped in Perth.

# Consonance

## But Outer Space by Robert Frost

But outer Space,

At least this far,

For all the fuss

Of the populace

Stays more popular

Than populous

## Over in the Meadow by Olive Wadsworth

Over in the meadow,

In the sand, in the sun,

Lived an old mother toad

And her little toadie one.

"Wink!" said the mother;

"I wink," said the one:

So she winked and she blinked

In the sand, in the sun.

# Consonance

## Frank by Lorrie L. Birchall

Frank may be a little skunk,
but he can make you blink.
When he lifts his chunky tail—
he makes a great big stink!

## Butterfly by Benjamin Franklin

What is a butterfly?
At best
He's but a caterpillar
Dressed.

## A Silly Little Mule by LeRoy F. Jackson

A silly little mule
Sat on a milking stool
And tried to write a letter to his father.
But he couldn't find the ink,
So he said: "I rather think
This writing letters home is too much bother."

# Consonance

## The Butter Betty Bought by Carolyn Wells

Betty Botta bought some butter;

"But," said she, "this butter's bitter!

If I put it in my batter

It will make my batter bitter.

But a bit o' better butter

will make my batter better."

Then she bought a bit o' butter

Better than the bitter butter,

Made her bitter batter better.

So 'twas better Betty Botta

bought a bit o' better butter.

(This poem is a good example of both **consonance** *and* **alliteration!**)

## The Fiddler by W.K. Clifford

The fiddler played upon his fiddle

All through that leafy June,

He always played hey-diddle-diddle,

And played it out of tune.

# Consonance

## Little Trotty Wagtail by John Clare

Little trotty wagtail, he went in the rain,

And tittering, tottering sideways he ne'er got straight again,

He stooped to get a worm, and looked up to get a fly,

And then he flew away ere his feathers they were dry.


Little trotty wagtail, he waddled in the mud,

And left his little footmarks, trample where he would.

He waddled in the water-pudge, and waggle went his tail,

And chirrupt up his wings to dry upon the garden rail.


Little trotty wagtail, you nimble all about,

And in the dimpling water-pudge you waddle in and out;

Your home is nigh at hand, and in the warm pig-stye,

So, little Master Wagtail, I'll bid you a good-bye.


## The Cardinal by Elizabeth Gordan

Cardinal bird wears vivid red,

He's very amiable, 'tis said;

He likes fresh fruits and seeds to eat

And has a song that's very sweet.

# What is Creative or "Poetic" License?

Poets like to play with words and language in fun and unusual ways.
When they take creative license, they intentionally
break language rules for creative effect.

Poets use creative license by:

- making up words

- using unusual spelling

- using unusual phrasing, capitalization, or punctuation

- using an unusual structure in a poem

- playing with syntax by ordering words in an unusual way

In the following poem, the poet took creative license by using a fun play on words
and unusual spelling.

# A Fellow From the Amazon by Unknown

A fellow from the Amazon,

Put nighties of his Gra'mazon.

The reason, that

He was too fat

To get his own pajamazon.

# Creative License

## My Feet by Gelett Burgess

My feet they haul me 'round the house;
They hoist me up the stairs;
I only have to steer them and
They ride me everywheres.

## The Ptarmigan by Unknown

The ptarmigan is strange,
As strange as he can be;
Never sits on ptelephone poles
Or roosts upon a ptree.
And the way he ptakes pto spelling
Is the strangest thing pto me.

## Four Seasons by Unknown

Spring is showery, flowery, bowery.
Summer: hoppy, choppy, poppy.
Autumn: wheezy, sneezy, freezy.
Winter: slippy, drippy, nippy.

# Creative License

## Why Wolves Howl by Unknown

Gray wolves do not howl at the moon.

Across a vast

timber

zone,

they oboe in

mono-

tone,

Fur-face, I am

all a-

lone.

## Uncle Simon and Uncle Jim by Artemus Ward

Uncle Simon he

Clum up a tree

To see what he could see

When presentlee

Uncle Jim

Clum up beside of him

And squatted down by he.

# Creative License

## The Cameleopard by Hilaire Belloc

The Cameleopard it is said
(By travelers who never lie),
He cannot stretch out straight in bed
Because he is so high.

The clouds surround his lofty head,
His hornlets touch the sky.
How shall I find this quadroped?
I shall not tell! Not I!

## Bull and Ox by Unknown

A *bull* acts like a bully
with a running start.
The ox enjoys a pull. He
tows any plow or cart.
One of them is slow and dull,
Both of them are large.
One is unpredictabull—
He's the one in . . .
                charge!

57

# Creative License

## Latitudes and Longitudes by Hugh Lofting

'Twas in the tropic latitudes

That we were talking platitudes,

Just sailor-like chit-chatitudes,

As any ship-mates might.

We forgot to take our longitude

(Which was a grievous wrongitude)

So we didn't reach Hong-kongitude

Till very late that night.

## The Toffee Analyst by Hugh Lofting

Oh, I'm the Toffee Analyst

So learned and sophisticky;

I'm making out a candy list,

It's going to be statisticky.

## Ketchup by Unknown

If you do not shake the bottle

None'll come and then, a lot'll.

# Creative License

## A Nursery Rhyme Mash-Up by Michael Lewis

Little Jack Horner sat in the corner
    Eyeing the pies all day,
While little Miss Muffet sat on her tuffet
    Eating her curds and whey.

Old Mother Hubbard then went to the cupboard
    To give him a pie and bun,
When out walked a spider and sat down beside her—
    So this little pig had none!

## Three Ghostesses by Unknown

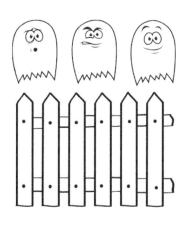

Three little ghostesses,
Sitting on postesses,
Eating buttered toastesses,
Greasing their fistesses,
Up to their wristesses,
Oh, what beastesses
To make such feastesses!

# What is an Elegy?

An elegy (pronounced ĕl-ĭ-jee) is a sad poem
usually written to express feelings of loss and sorrow
for someone who has died.

Louisa May Alcott wrote this elegy about her pet cat, Snowball.

## Snowball by Louisa May Alcott

We mourn the loss of our little pet,
And sigh o'er her hapless fate,
For never more by the fire she'll sit,
Nor play by the old green gate.

Her empty bed, her idle ball,
Will never see her more;
No gentle tap, no loving purr
Is heard at the parlor door.

Another cat comes after her mice,
A cat with a dirty face,
But she does not hunt as our darling did,
Nor play with her airy grace.

Her stealthy paws tread the very hall
Where Snowball used to play,
But she only spits at the dogs our pet
So gallantly drove away.

She is useful and mild, and does her best,
But she is not fair to see,
And we cannot give her your place dear,
Nor worship her as we worship thee.

**Louisa May Alcott** (1832 – 1888) was an American novelist, short story writer,
and poet best known as the author of the novel *Little Women* (1868) and its sequels.

# What is an Epitaph?

An epitaph (pronounced **ĕp**-ĭ-taff) is a phrase or statement written

in memory of a person who has died,

usually as an inscription written on a tombstone.

Some epitaphs are humorous like the ones below.

## Epitaph for My Wife

Here lies my wife: Here let her lie!

Now she's at rest, and so am I!

## Ann Jennings

Some have children, some have none;

Here lies the mother of twenty-one.

## Marcus Bent

Here lies the body of Marcus Bent.

He kicked up his heels, and away he went.

# Epitaphs

## Remember, Friend

Remember, friend, as you pass by,
As you are now, so once was I;
As I am now thus you must be,
So be prepared to follow me.

## Mushrooms

I thought it mushroom when I found
It in the woods, forsaken;
But since I sleep beneath this mound,
I must have been mistaken.

## Matthew Mudd

Here lies Matthew Mudd,
Death did him no hurt;
When alive he was Mudd
Now he's nothing but dirt.

## Ann Mann

Here lies the body of Ann Mann,
Who lived an old woman,
And died an old Mann.

# Epitaphs

## Tom Thumb's Epitaph by Unknown

Here lies Tom Thumb, King Arthur's Knight,

Who died by a spider's cruel bite.

He was well known in Arthur's court,

Where he afforded gallant sport.

He rode at tilt and tournament,

And on a mouse-hunting went.

Alive he filled the court with mirth;

His death to sorrow soon gave birth.

Wipe, wipe your eyes and shake your head

And cry—alas! Tom Thumb is dead.

# Epitaphs

## Here Lies Fred by Unknown

Here lies Fred,

Who was alive, but now is dead.

If it had been his father,

I would much rather;

If it had been his brother,

Still better than another;

If it had been his sister,

No one would have missed her;

If it had been the whole generation,

So much the better for the nation.

But as it's only Fred,

Who was alive, but now is dead,

Why there's no more to be said.

# Epitaphs

In 1728, as a twenty-two year old young man,
Benjamin Franklin wrote his own mock (pretend) epitaph:

## Benjamin Franklin

The Body of B. Franklin (Printer)

Like the Cover of an old Book

Its contents torn out,

And stript of its Lettering and Gilding

Lies here, Food for Worms.

But the Work shall not be wholly lost

For it will, as he believed,

Appear once more

In a new and more perfect Edition

Corrected and Amended

by the Author.

He was born on January 6, 1706.

Died 17_ _

Benjamin Franklin (1706-1790) died at 84 years of age.

His actual grave simply reads, Benjamin and Deborah Franklin, 1790

# What is Eye Rhyme?

Eye rhyme occurs when two words *look* like they should rhyme
due to their spelling, but they don't *sound* like a truc rhyme.
For this reason, eye rhymes are also called *spelling rhymes.*

Poets use eye rhymes:

- to be unexpected

- to open up more word choice

- to reduce the predictable sing-song of a true rhyme.

Examples of eye rhymes:

come/home

cough/bough

laughter/daughter

love/move

bone/none

# Old Mother Hubbard -Traditional Nursery Rhyme

Old Mother Hubbard
Went to the cupboard,
To give her poor dog a **bone**;
But when she got there
The cupboard was bare,
And so the poor dog had **none**.

# Eye Rhyme

## Tis the Last Rose of Summer by Thomas Moore

Tis the last rose of summer

Left blooming alone;

All her lovely companions

Are faded and gone.

## Old Mother Goose -Traditional Nursery Rhyme

Old Mother Goose, when

She wanted to wander,

Would ride through the air

On a very fine gander.

## At Home by George MacDonald

The lightning and thunder

They go and they come:

But the stars and the stillness

Are always at home.

# Eye Rhyme

## Mrs. Spider by Katherine Forrest Hamill

Brother Dan and I one day
Watched Mrs. Spider spin away;
My, how she spun, and spun, and spun,
Until she had her web all done!

Then brother Dan, he said to me:
"Now, where can Mr. Spider be?"
We watched, but didn't see him come,
So I guess he didn't live at home.

## When the Snow is on the Ground

-Traditional Nursery Rhyme

The little robin grieves
    When the snow is on the ground,
For the trees have no leaves,
    And no berries can be found.

The air is cold, the worms are hid;
    For robin here what can be done?
Let's throw around some crumbs of bread,
    And then he'll live till snow is gone.

# Eye Rhyme

## To a Squirrel by William Butler Yeats

Come play with me;
Why should you run
Through the shaking tree
As though I'd a gun
To strike you dead?
When all I would do
Is to scratch your head
And let you go.

## The Hedgehog by Edith King

The hedgehog is a little beast
Who likes a quiet wood,
Where he can feed his family
On proper hedgehog food.

He does not need to battle with
Or run away from foes,
His coat does all the work for him,
It pricks them on the nose.

# What is a Fable Poem?

A fable poem is a story poem that is meant to teach a lesson.

Many are based on Aesop's fables,

which often have animal (anthropomorphic) characters

and a moral at the end.

## The Ant and the Cricket by Unknown

A silly young cricket, accustomed to sing

Through the warm, sunny months of the summer and spring,

Began to complain, when he found that at home

His cupboard was empty and winter had come.

    Not a crumb to be found

    on the snow covered ground;

    Not a flower could he see,

    Not a leaf on a tree:

"Oh, what will become," said the cricket, "of me?"

At last by starvation and famine made bold,

All dripping with wet and all trembling with cold,

Away he set off to a miserly ant,

To see if, to keep him alive, he would grant

    Him shelter from rain:

    A mouthful of grain

    He wished only to borrow,

    He'd repay it tomorrow:

If not, he must die of starvation and sorrow.

Says the ant to the cricket, "I'm your servant and friend,

But we ants never borrow, we ants never lend;

But tell me, dear sir, did you lay nothing by

When the weather was warm?" said the cricket, "Not I,

      My heart was so light

      That I sang day and night,

      For all nature looked gay."

      "You *sang*, sir, you say?

Go then," said the ant, "and *dance* winter away."

*It is important to prepare for days of necessity.*

# Fable Poem

## The Lion and the Mouse by Lorrie L. Birchall

When Lion reached out with his claw,

He couldn't believe what he saw,

A mousy good treat,

That he'd like to eat,

Just sitting right there in his paw.

The Mouse made a vigorous plea,

If Lion would only agree,

"If you'll let me go,

a favor I'll owe,

to help you—whenever need be."

The Lion just laughed at the thought,

But let the Mouse go, and forgot.

The Mouse ran away,

Without a delay,

And Lion walked off in a trot.

Soon Lion was caught in a net,

Which certainly made him upset.

The Mouse heard his roar,

And didn't ignore,

The promise to pay off his debt.


He ran to the Lion distraught,

And chewed through the ropes on the spot.

The Lion went free,

So Mouse helped him see,

A little help means quite a lot.


*A little help can make a big difference in outcome.*


# The Tortoise and the Hare by Lorrie L. Birchall

When Tortoise and Hare had a race,

It seemed like a very slow pace.

So Hare took a nap,

Instead of a lap,

And Tortoise took home the first place.

*Talent doesn't guarantee outcome.*

73

# Fable Poem

## The Fox and the Grapes by Lorrie L. Birchall

When Fox noticed grapes on a vine,

He thought he was going to dine,

    But the grapes were up high,

    So he leaped in the sky,

But fell to the ground with a whine.


He gazed at the grapes in their prime,

But groused it was not worth the climb,

    "The grapes must be sour,

    And bad to devour,

And certainly not worth my time."


*It's easy to pretend to dislike that which is beyond your reach.*

# Fable Poem

## The Crow and the Water Jar by Oliver Herford

Thirsty Crow once found a Jar
That held some water, but 'twas far

Too narrow necked, and much too low
The water was, for Master Crow

With his short neck to get a drink.
The Crow then set himself to think—

At last upon a plan he hit.
"Since I cannot reach down to it,

I must invent some way," said he,
"To make the water rise to me."

With little pebbles, one by one,
He filled the Jar; as this was done

The water rose and rose, until
The thirsty Crow could drink his fill.

*When there is a will, there is a way.*

# Fable Poem

## The Fox and the Crow by Jane Taylor

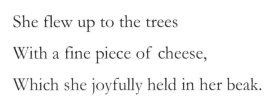

To a dairy, a crow

Once ventured to go,

Some food for her young ones to seek.


She flew up to the trees

With a fine piece of cheese,

Which she joyfully held in her beak.

A fox, who near by,

To the tree saw her fly,

And to share in the prize made a vow;


For, having just dined,

He for cheese felt inclined,

So he went and sat under the bough.


She was cunning, he knew,

But so was he, too,

And to flatter adapted his plan.


If the crow should try to speak

The cheese must fall from her beak—

So, politely, then, the fox began:

"'Tis a very fine day,"

(Not a word did she say):

"The wind, I believe, ma'am is south;

A fine harvest for peas."

He then looked at the cheese,

But the crow did not open her mouth.

Sly Reynard, not tired,

Her plumage admired:

"How charming! How brilliant its hue!

The voice must be fine,

Of a bird so divine—

Ah, let me just hear it, please do!

Believe me, I long

To hear a sweet song."

The silly crow foolishly tries:

She scarce gives one squall

When the cheese she lets fall,

And the fox runs away with the prize.

*Don't let flattery cloud your judgement.*

# Fable Poem

## Belling the Cat by Oliver Herford

Once, in the absence of the Cat,

The Mice in solemn council sat,

Some plan of action to discuss

To curb her practice odious

Of prying into their affairs

And pouncing on them unawares.

After much talk the plan that met

With most approval was to get

A piece of rope and hang thereby

To Kitty's neck, upon the sly,

A bell that would not fail to ring

When Kitty was about to spring,

And so announce her full intention.

Truly a wonderful invention!

The Mice delightedly agreed.

"Now," said the Chairman, "all we need

Is someone to attach the bell."

At this, an awful silence fell

Upon the meeting; no one spoke.

At length a voice the stillness broke,

"I move, since no one seems to yearn

To bell the Cat, that we adjourn."

*Having ideas is not the same as following them through.*

# Fable Poem

## The Crab and His Mother by Oliver Herford

Said a Crab in tone irate

To her son, "Your sidelong gait

Annoys me—can you not go straight?"

Said the Son, "I'll try, if you

Will show me how." What could she do?

Mother Crab went sideways too!

*An example teaches more than words.*

## The Dog and His Shadow by Oliver Herford

A Dog, with a choice bit of meat

That he was carrying home to eat,

Crossing a bridge, saw in the brook

His own reflection, which he took

To be another Dog. "The Pig!

His piece of meat is twice as big

As mine! Well, I'll soon let him see

Which is the better Dog!" cried he;

And dropping his, without ado,

To grab the other's meat he flew.

Meanwhile his own sank out of sight;

Thus he lost both, which served him right!"

*Greed does not help you appreciate what you have.*

79

# Fable Poem

## The Dog and the Wolf by Oliver Herford

A lazy Dog that sleeping lay

Outside the farmyard gate, one day,

Woke with a sudden start, to see

A fierce Wolf glaring hungrily,

Gruesome and grisly, gaunt and grim,

And just about to spring on him.

"Oh Wolf!" exclaimed the frightened Pup,

"One word before you eat me up!

Observe how very small and thin

I am; 'twould really be a sin

To eat me now.  Indeed I'm quite

Unworthy of your appetite.

Tomorrow Master gives a treat,

And I shall have so much to eat

That if you'll wait a day or two

I'll make a bigger meal for you!"

The wolf agreed and went away;

But when on the appointed day

He came again to claim his right,

He found the farmyard gate shut tight,

And Doggie on the other side.

"What does this mean? Come out!" he cried.

Loud laughed the Dog, "It means," said he,

"I'm wiser than I used to be!"

*Experience is a great teacher.*

# What is Free Verse?

Free verse is not restricted to follow poetry "rules"
or identifiable meter and rhyme schemes.

It's *free* to do what it wants.

Free Verse doesn't use:

- consistent meter patterns

- rhyme

- or any other musical pattern

## A Farm Picture by Walt Whitman

Through the ample open door of the peaceful country barn,
A sun-lit pasture field, with cattle and horses feeding;
And haze, and vista, and the far horizon, fading away.

## Poems by Hilda Conkling

Poems come like boats
With sails for wings;
Crossing the sky swiftly
They slip under tall bridges
Of cloud.

81

# Free Verse

## Butterfly by Hilda Conkling

Butterfly,

I like the way you wear your wings.

Show me their colors,

For the light is going.

Spread out their edges of gold,

Before the Sandman puts me to sleep

And evening murmurs by.

## By Lake Champlain by Hilda Conkling

I was bare as a leaf

And I felt the wind on my shoulder.

The trees laughed

When I picked up the sun in my fingers.

The wind was chasing the waves,

Tangling their white curls.

"Willow trees," I said, "O willows,

Look at your lake!

Stop laughing at a little girl

Who runs past your feet in the sand!"

# Free Verse

## The Thunder Shower by Hilda Conkling

The dark cloud raged.

Gone was the morning light.

The big drops darted down:

The storm stood tall on the rose-trees:

And the bees were getting honey

Out of wet roses.

The hiding bees would not come out of the flowers

Into the rain.

## After Many Springs by Langston Hughes

Now,

in June,

When the night is a vast softness

Filled with blue stars,

And broken shafts of moon-glimmer

Fall upon the earth,

Am I too old to see the fairies dance?

I cannot find them any more.

# Free Verse

## A Sphinx by Carl Sandburg

Close-mouthed you sat five thousand years and never

let out a whisper.

Processions came by, marchers, asking questions you

answered with grey eyes never blinking, shut lips

never talking.

Not one croak of anything you know has come from your

cat crouch of ages.

I am one of those who know all you know and I keep my

questions: I know the answers you hold.

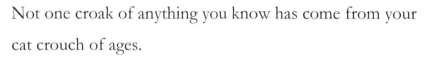

## Soup by Carl Sandburg

I saw a famous man eating soup.

I say he was lifting a fat broth

Into his mouth with a spoon.

His name was in the newspapers that day

Spelled out in tall black headlines

And thousands of people were talking about him.

When I saw him,

He sat bending his head over a plate

Putting soup in his mouth with a spoon.

# Free Verse

## The Locust by Unknown

Your hot voice sizzles from some cool tree nearby:

You seem to burn your way through the air

Like a small pointed flame of sound

Sharpened on the ecstatic edge of sunbeams!

## Your Voice by Amy Lowell

Your voice is like bells over roofs at dawn

When a bird flies

And the sky changes to a fresher color.

## Ships in the Harbor by John Gould Fletcher

Like a flock of great blue cranes

Resting upon the water,

The ships assemble at morning,

when the gray light wakes in the east.

(Bonus: Can you identify the **similes** in each of the poems above?)

# Free Verse

## Storm by H.D.

You crash over the trees,

you crack the live branch—

the branch is white,

the green crushed,

each leaf is rent like split wood.

You burden the trees

with black drops,

you swirl and crash—

you have broken off a weighted leaf

in the wind,

it is hurled out,

whirls up and inks,

a green stone.

## When the Rain Falls by John Gould Fletcher

When the rain falls,

I watch sliver spears slanting downwards

From the pale river pools of sky,

Enclosed in dark fronds.

# Free Verse

## Elves Go Fetch Your Lanterns by Rachel Field

Elves, go fetch your lanterns:

Light up every pine cone

Where the woods are thickest,

Lest, when darkness falls

Black as any witch-cloak,

Baby birds should wake and cry

Fearful in the dark.

## Wind and Silver by Amy Lowell

Greatly shining,

The Autumn moon floats in the thin sky;

And the fish-ponds shake their backs and flash their dragon scales

As she passes over them

# What is Hyperbole?

Hyperbole (pronounced hī-**per**-bōlee)

is extreme exaggeration.

Example:

I ate a million hot dogs.

(Could you *really* eat a million hot dogs…or are you **exaggerating**?)

## Hot Dogs for Breakfast by Lorrie L. Birchall

I woke up feeling famished,

but cereal is dull.

I ate a million hot dogs,

so now I'm really full!

## Freckles by Rachel Field

Jane's hair is gold as a daffodil.

Blue as the sea are the eyes of Will.

Nan's lips are redder than any rose—

But Rick has freckles on his nose,

Almost as many as I should say

As there are stars on the milky way!

# Hyperbole

## I Ate a Spicy Pepper by Unknown

I ate a spicy pepper

From my brother on a dare.

The pepper caught my head on fire

And burned off all my hair.


My mouth erupted lava

And my tongue began to melt.

My ears were shooting jets of steam.

At least that's how they felt.

I ricocheted around the room.

I ran across the ceiling.

I dove right in the freezer

To relieve the burning feeling.


I drank a thousand soda pops

And chewed a ton of ice

To try to stop the scorching

Of that spicy pepper's spice.


At last, the flames extinguished,

I admitted to my brother,

"That pepper was the best one yet.

May I please have another?"

# Hyperbole

## Terrible Tim by LeRoy F. Jackson

Haven't you heard of Terrible Tim?

Well, don't you get in the way of him.

He eats lions for breakfast

And leopards for lunch,

And gobbles them down

With one terrible crunch.

He could mix a whole city

All up in a mess,

He could drink up a sea

Or an ocean, I guess.

You'd better be watching for Terrible Tim,

And run when you first get your peepers on him.

## Summer by Ralph Bergengren

Some days are hot, and after showers,

You smell a million, million flowers.

And when no shower comes and goes,

I make one with the garden hose.

# Hyperbole

## The Quangle Wangle's Hat by Edward Lear

On the top of the Crumpetty tree
The Quangle Wangle sat,
But his face you could not see,
On account of his beaver hat.

For his hat was a hundred and two feet wide,
With ribbons and bibbons on every side,
And bells, and buttons, and loops, and lace,
So that nobody ever could see the face
Of the Quangle Wangle Quee.

## The Young Lady with a Nose by Edward Lear

There was a young lady whose nose,
Was so long that it reached to her toes;
    So she hired an old lady,
    Whose conduct was steady,
To carry that wonderful nose.

# Hyperbole

## The Old Woman Tossed Up in a Basket

-Traditional Nursery Rhyme

There was an old woman tossed up in a basket,
Seventeen times as high as the moon;
Where she was going I could not but ask it,
For in her hand she carried a broom.

"Old woman, old woman, old woman," said I;
"O whither, O whither, O whither so high?"
"To sweep the cobwebs from the sky,
 And I'll be with you by-and-by!"

## The Elk by Ruth McEnery Stuart & Albert Bigelow Paine

Look at the head of the elk and you'll see,
His horns are as tall as a sycamore tree.
They are strangely designed,
And I think you will find,
He has horns where his ears ought to be.

# What is Imagery?

Poets intentionally choose interesting words
to help create strong pictures in your head.
Even very short poems can create vivid mental images
through powerful word choice.

Poets create imagery by using:

- descriptive words—especially vivid adjectives & action verbs

- sensory words—appealing to sight, smell, taste, touch & sound

- figurative language—such as similes, metaphors, personification, onomatopoeia, etc.

# Broadway in a Fog by John Richard Moreland

Grotesque shadows of vehicles and people

Gliding over smooth asphalt,

Gray mists blotting out the towering buildings

While the yellow lights

In the high windows

Are like fireflies

Caught in a net of silver.

What descriptive words did the poet choose to help create vivid imagery?

# Imagery

## The Juggler of Day by Emily Dickinson

Blazing in gold and quenching in purple,

Leaping like leopards to the sky,

Then at the feet of the old horizon

Laying her spotted face, to die;

Stooping as low as the otter's window,

Touching the roof and tinting the barn,

Kissing her bonnet to the meadow—

And the juggler of day is gone!

## Sunset by Emily Dickinson

Where ships of purple gently toss

On seas of daffodil,

Fantastic sailors mingle,

And then—the wharf is still.

## Symphony by L. H. Bailey

The leaves upon the Aspen tree

They poppled in the breeze

and held the drifting harmony

of music in the trees.

# Imagery

## The Seagull -Gaelic Folk Song

All day long o'er the ocean I fly,

My white wings beating fast through the sky,

I hunt fishes all down the bay

And ride on rocking billows in play.


All night long in my rock home I rest,

Away up on a cliff is my nest,

The waves murmur, murmur below,

And winds fresh from the sea o'er me blow.

## After Darkness by Oliver Jenkins

Sitting in the darkness

After sunset

Is a wondertime

When memories hover and tremble

Like deep glowing painted lanterns

Flickering in the wind.

# Imagery

## Summer Evening by Walter de la Mare

The sandy cat by the farmer's chair

Mews at his knee for dainty fare;

Old Rover in his moss-greened house,

Mumbles a bone, and barks at a mouse.


In the dewy fields the cattle lie

Chewing the cud 'neath a fading sky.

Dobbin at manger pulls his hay:

Gone is another summer's day.

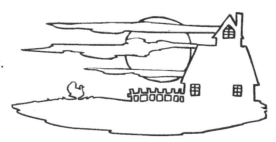

## Slippery by Carl Sandburg

The sixth month child

Fresh from the tub

Wriggles in our hands.

This is our fish child.

Give her a nickname: Slippery.

# Imagery

## Alley Cat by Esther Valck Georges

A bit of jungle in the street
He goes on velvet toes,
And slinking through the shadows, stalks
Imaginary foes.

## The Wolf Cry by Lew Sarett

The Arctic moon hangs overhead;
The wide white silence lies below.
A starveling pine stands lone and gaunt,
Black-penciled on the snow.
Weird as the moan of sobbing winds,
A lone long call floats up from the trail;
And the naked soul of the frozen North
Trembles in that wail.

# Imagery

## Elves and Apple Trees by Rachel Field

Elves love best of all to run

Through old orchards in the sun,

By gnarled and twisted apple trees

With crooked arms and knobbly knees,

With roots like humps, and leaves like hair,

And twigs that clutch and claw the air.

They help to hang the blossoms out

And in the fall, oh, never doubt

When apples shine above your head

It was some elf who made them red!

## The Mirror by A.A. Milne

Between the woods the afternoon

Is fallen in a golden swoon,

The sun looks down from quiet skies

To where a quiet water lies,

    And silent trees stoop down to trees.

And there I saw a white swan make

Another white swan in the lake.

And, breast to breast, both motionless,

They waited for the wind's caress…

    And all the water was at ease.

# Imagery

## Logic by Rowena Bastin Bennett

Into the pocket of the night,

The red sun dropped

    like a penny, bright;

The round moon rose

    like a silver dime,

Is that what they mean

    by "spending time?"

## Evening: New York by Sara Teasdale

Blue dust of evening over my city,

Over the ocean of roofs and the tall towers

Where the window-lights, myriads and myriads,

Bloom from the walls like climbing flowers.

# What is Inference?

We use clues from text & illustrations

to make an inference (draw a conclusion in our head),

even when not all the information is given.


Example:

"Sara was yawning and yawning when she got home from work."

Although it isn't specifically stated, we can *infer* that Sara is likely feeling tired.


## Crocodile Pet by Unknown

I had a crocodile

for a pet.

Unfortunately, no one's

found me yet.

(Can you *infer* what happened to the pet owner?)


## Pet Vampire Bat by Lorrie L. Birchall

I have a new pet,

a blood-sucking bat.

Now why is he looking

at me like that?


(Can you *infer* why the bat is looking that way?)

# Inference

## Spoilers by Emma Rounds

Once we lived in fairyland
With mysteries on every hand;
We had a dungeon dark and deep
Where wicked prisoners we'd keep.

The loveliest prince, we had there, too,
With a beautiful princess for him to woo;
We put her up in a tower stout—
And we were the fairies who got her out!

There was a fairy King and Queen
With palaces and everything!
And we had ladies, fair and knights,
Who had the most exciting fights!

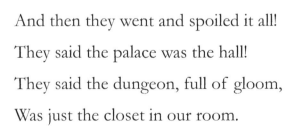

And then they went and spoiled it all!
They said the palace was the hall!
They said the dungeon, full of gloom,
Was just the closet in our room.

Can you *infer* who the spoilers might be?
Can you *infer* who is telling the story?

# Inference

## The Transferred Smile

by Ruth McEnery Stuart & Albert Bigelow Paine

Two little snails did smile and smile,
The summer day beguiling.
Two birds espied them from afar,
And now the birds are smiling.

(Can you *infer* why the birds are now smiling?)

## A Puzzle by Unknown

The man in the wilderness asked of me
'How many strawberries grow in the sea?'
I answered him as I thought good,
'As many fishes as grow in the wood.'

(Can you *infer* the answer?)

# Inference

## When Ice Cream Grows on Spaghetti Trees
by Unknown

When ice cream grows on spaghetti trees,

And the Sahara Desert grows muddy,

When cats and dogs wear underwear

That's the time to study.

(According to the poem, can you *infer* when it's a good time to study?)

## Crocodile by Unknown

If you should meet a crocodile

Don't take a stick and poke him;

Ignore the welcome in his smile,

Be careful not to stroke him.

For as he sleeps upon the Nile,

He thinner gets and thinner;

Whenever you meet a crocodile

He's looking for his dinner.

(Can you *infer* what the crocodile wants for his dinner?)

# Inference

## The Young Man from the City by Unknown

There was a young man from the city,

Who met what he thought was a kitty,

    He gave it a pat,

    And said, "Nice little cat!"

And they buried his clothes out of pity.

(Can you *infer* what happened to the young man?)

## The Chameleon by Carolyn Wells

The true Chameleon is small,

    A lizard sort of thing:

He hasn't any ears at all,

    And not a single wing.

If there is nothing on the tree,

    'Tis the Chameleon you see.

(What can you *infer* about a Chameleon?)

# What is Internal Rhyme?

Internal rhyme occurs when two words rhyme
*inside* the same line.

Example:

That poetry **line** is simply **divine**.

## Little Jack Horner -Traditional Nursery Rhyme

Little Jack **Horner** sat in a **corner**,

Eating a Christmas pie;

He put in his **thumb**, and pulled out a **plum**,

And said, "What a good boy am I!"

## Jack and Jill -Traditional Nursery Rhyme

Jack and **Jill** went up the **hill**

To fetch a pail of water;

Jack fell **down** and broke his **crown**,

And Jill came tumbling after.

# Internal Rhyme

## Cross Patch -Traditional Nursery Rhyme

Cross patch, draw the latch,
Sit by the fire and spin;
Take a cup and drink it up,
Then call your neighbors in.

## Hark! Hark! -Traditional Nursery Rhyme

Hark, hark! The dogs do bark!
Beggars are coming to town:
Some in jags, and some in rags,
And some in velvet gown.

## Advice by Unknown

Don't shirk your work
for the sake of a dream.
A fish in the dish
is worth two in the stream.

# Internal Rhyme

## Little Bo-Peep -Traditional Nursery Rhyme

Little Bo-Peep, she lost her sheep,
And didn't know where to find them;
Let them alone, they'll all come home
And bring their tails behind them.

Little Bo-Peep fell fast asleep,
And dreamt she heard them bleating;
But when she awoke, she found it a joke,
For they were still a-fleeting.

Then up she took her little crook,
Determined yet to find them,
She found them indeed, but it made her heart bleed
For they'd left their tails behind them.

It happened one day as Bo-Peep did stray
Into a meadow hard by,
There she espied their tails side by side,
All hung on a tree to dry.

She heaved a sigh and wiped her eye,
Then went o'er hill and dale,
And tried what she could, as a shepherdess should,
To tack to each sheep its tail.

Bonus: Can you find the *near rhyme* in the first stanza?

# Internal Rhyme

## The Rainy Day by Evaleen Stein

Let's sail all day, away, away

To the splendid Spanish Main

And the sultry seas of the Caribbees

And skies that never rain!

As pirates bold with bags of gold

And cutlasses and things,

We'll pack doubloons and silver spoons

In chests with iron rings.

And these we'll carry and secretly bury

In cannibal isles afar;

Like Captain Kidd, when they're safely hid

We won't tell where they are.

Let's sail all day, away, away

To the splendid Spanish Main

And the sultry seas of the Caribbees—

But at night sail home again.

# Internal Rhyme

## A Camel's Back by Lorrie L. Birchall

Lumpy, bumpy camel's back,
A challenge to command;
Braying, swaying to and fro
across a land of sand.

## A Nook and a Storybook -Old English Song

Oh, for a nook and a storybook,
With tales both new and old;
For a jolly good book upon to look
Is better to me than gold.

## Old Mister McNether by LeRoy F. Jackson

Old Mister McNether sorts out the weather
And takes what he pleases, I'm told,
With a big turkey feather, he mixes the weather,
And makes it blow hot and blow cold.

# Internal Rhyme

## Upon the Irish Sea by LeRoy F. Jackson

Someone told Maria Ann,

Maria Ann told me,

That kittens ride in coffee cans

Upon the Irish Sea.

From quiet caves to rolling waves,

How jolly it must be

To travel in a coffee can

Upon the Irish Sea!

But when it snows and when it blows,

How would you like to be

A kitten in a coffee can

Upon the Irish Sea?

## Fuzzy Wuzzy by Unknown

Fuzzy Wuzzy was a bear,

Fuzzy Wuzzy had no hair,

Fuzzy Wuzzy wasn't fuzzy,

Was he?

# Internal Rhyme

## Under the Willow by LeRoy F. Jackson

Put down your pillow under the willow,

Hang up your hat in the sun,

And lie down to snooze as long as you choose,

For the plowing and sowing are done.

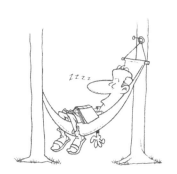

Pick up your pillow from under the willow,

And clamber out into the sun.

Get a fork and a rake for goodness' sake,

For the harvest time has begun.

## The Mermaidens by Laura E. Richards

The little mermaidens all live in the sea,

In a palace of silver and gold.

And their neat little tails are all covered in scales,

Most beautiful for to behold.

On wild sea horses they ride, they ride,

In chairs of pink coral they sit;

They swim all the night, with a smile of delight,

And never feel tired one bit.

# What is a Metaphor?

A metaphor says (or implies) that one thing **is** something else.

It doesn't use the words "like" or "as" the way similes do.

Example:

Fame **is** a bee.        (metaphor)

Fame **is like** a bee. (simile)

## Fame is a Bee by Emily Dickinson

Fame is a bee.

It has a song—

It has a sting—

Ah, too, it has a wing.

There is another important difference between similes and metaphors in poetry.

Unlike a simile, an entire poem can act as a metaphor.

In the poem, "The Land of Nod," the entire poem is a metaphor for sleep.

# Metaphor

## The Land of Nod by Robert Louis Stevenson

From breakfast on all through the day
At home among my friends I stay;
But every night I go abroad
Afar into the land of Nod.

All by myself I have to go,
With none to tell me what to do—
All alone beside the streams
And up the mountain-sides of dreams.

The strangest things are there for me,
Both things to eat and things to see,
And many frightening sights abroad
Till morning in the land of Nod.

Try as I like to find the way,
I never can get back by day,
Nor can remember plain and clear
The curious music that I hear.

# Metaphor

## Sleep by John B. Tabb

When he is a little chap,

    We call him *Nap.*

When he somewhat older grows,

    We call him *Doze.*

When his age by hours we number,

    We call him *Slumber.*

## Happiness is a Perfume by Unknown

Happiness is a perfume

You cannot pour it on others

Without getting a few drops on yourself.

## A Modern Dragon by Rowena Bastin Bennett

A train is a dragon that roars through the dark.

He wriggles his tail as he sends up a spark.

He pierces the night with his one yellow eye,

And all the earth trembles as he rushes by.

# Metaphor

## Bread by Ethel Romig Fuller

Wheat is still. It makes no sound
As it pushes from the ground.

As it runs it's slow, serene
Course in rows of tender green.

Wheat is quiet, as it grows
It only whispers what it knows.

Wheat is mute—till it is fed
To children as a loaf of bread.

Then it is laughter; it is song;
It is clamor all day long.

## Butter by Ethel Romig Fuller

Butter is music of wind that passes
Through blue alfalfa and supple grasses.

It is sun on meadows, it is lyric notes
Of rain and honey on clover throats.

It is the pale gold rhythmic tread
Of summer on a slice of bread.

115

# Metaphor

## A Song of Popcorn by Nancy Byrd Turner

Sing a song of popcorn
When the snowstorms rage;
Fifty little gold men
Put into a cage.

Shake them till they laugh and leap
Crowding to the top;
Watch them burst their little coats!
Pop! Pop! Pop!

Sing a song of popcorn
In the firelight;
Fifty little fairies
Robed in fleecy white.

## Daffodowndilly by A.A. Milne

She wore her yellow sun-bonnet,
She wore her greenest gown.
She turned to the south wind
And curtsied up and down.
She turned to the sunlight
And shook her yellow head,
And whispered to her neighbor:
*"Winter is dead."*

# Metaphor

## Pretty Dandelion by Unknown

There was a pretty dandelion
With lovely, fluffy hair,
That glistened in the sunshine
And in the summer air.

But oh, this pretty dandelion
Would soon get old and grey;
And, sad to tell, her charming hair
Blew many miles away.

## Dandelion by Hilda Conkling

Oh, little soldier with the golden helmet,
What are you guarding on my lawn?
You with your yellow beard,
Why do you stand so stiff?
There is only the grass to fight!

## The Pedigree of Honey by Emily Dickinson

The pedigree of honey
Does not concern the bee;
A clover, any time, to him,
Is aristocracy.

# Metaphor

## Nature's Poems and Music by Unknown

The flowers are Nature's poems,

in blue and red and gold.

With every change from bud to bloom

sweet fantasies unfold.

The trees are Nature's music—

Her living harps are they,

on which the fingers of the wind

majestic marches play.

## After Rain by Ethel Romig Fuller

Wet pavements

At night

Are black satin

Mandarin robes,

Stiff with embroidery

Of golden lilies,

And fiery, swirling

Dragon's tails.

# Metaphor

## Wind is a Cat by Ethel Romig Fuller

Wind is a cat
That prowls at night,
Now in a valley,
Now on a height,

Pouncing on houses
Till folks in their beds
Draw all the covers
Over their heads.

It sings to the moon,
It scratches at doors;
It lashes its tail
Around chimneys and roars.

It claws at the clouds
Till it fringes their silk,
It laps up the dawn
Like a saucer of milk;

Then, chasing the stars
To the tops of the firs,
Curls down for a nap
And purrs and purrs.

# Metaphor

## Clouds by Christina Georgina Rossetti

White sheep, white sheep

On a blue hill,

When the wind stops

You all stand still.

When the wind blows

You walk away slow.

White sheep, white sheep

Where do you go?

## The Clouds by Rowena Bastin Bennett

The clouds are birds that nest among the stars.

    They do not sing,

    But sleep with folded wing

Until the wind breaks through the shining bars

    Of morning, crying, "Come!"

    Then, slowly, one by one,

    They wake and fly

    Across the sky.

# Metaphor

## The Raindrops' Ride by Unknown

Some little drops of water
Whose home was in the sea,
To go upon a journey
Once happened to agree.

A white cloud was their carriage,
Their horse a playful breeze;
And over town and country
They rode along at ease.

But, oh! There were so many,
At last the carriage broke,
And to the ground came tumbling
Those frightened little folk.

Among the grass and flowers
They then were forced to roam,
Until a brooklet found them
And carried them all home.

# Metaphor

## The Rainbow Fairies by Unknown

Two little clouds, one summer's day,

Went flying through the sky;

They went so fast they bumped their heads,

And both began to cry.


Old Father Sun looked out and said:

"Oh never mind, my dears,

I'll send my little fairy folk

To dry your falling tears."


One fairy came in violet,

And one wore indigo;

In blue, green, yellow, orange, and red,

They made a pretty row.


They wiped the cloud-tears all away,

And then from out the sky,

Upon a light of sunbeams made,

They hung their gowns to dry.

# Metaphor

## The Rain by Rowena Bastin Bennett

The rain, they say, is a mouse-gray horse,

That is shod with a silver shoe;

The sound of his hoofs can be heard on the roofs

As he gallops the whole night through.

## Sky Matches by Abbie Farwell Brown

I wonder when the lightnings spark

And flicker from afar,

Who's scratching matches on the dark

To light some blown-out star?

## Snow by Rowena Bastin Bennett

Snow is a bird, soft-feathered and white.

Silent and graceful is her flight

As she swoops to earth and spreads her wings

Over the beautiful unborn things:

Seeds and bulbs that soon will tower

Out f the nest of the ground, and flower.

# Metaphor

## The Early Morning by Hilaire Belloc

The moon on the one hand, the dawn on the other:

The moon is my sister, the dawn is my brother.

The moon on my left and the dawn on my right.

My brother, good morning: my sister, good night.

## The New Day by William H. Simpson

The swift scouts of dawn ride in,

Their lances flame-tipped.

The waning moon shines whitely,

Like thin drifted snow—

And the cradled winds sleepily rub their eyes.

# Metaphor

## The Orange by Mary Carolyn Davies

The sky is a greedy child
Who holds one
Yellow orange in her hand:
It is the sun.

She holds it primly:
Then, hid from sight,
All in the darkness,
Eats it at night.

## A Sunset by Mary Carolyn Davies

Life seems so sweet! I don't know why—
Perhaps it's just because the sky
Put on tonight to make me glad,
A dress I didn't know she had.

## Ding Dong by Unknown

Ding-dong, the sun has gone:
A crimson nightgown he put on:
I saw him cover up his head:
Ding-dong, he's safe in bed.

# Metaphor

## An Indian Summer Day on the Prairie by Vachel Lindsey

(In the Beginning)

The sun is a huntress young,
The sun is a red, red joy,
The sun is an Indian girl,
Of the tribe of the Illinois.

(Mid-morning)

The sun is a smoldering fire,
That creeps through the high gray plain,
And leaves not a bush of cloud
To blossom with flowers of rain.

(Noon)

The sun is a wounded deer,
That treads pale grass in the skies,
Shaking his golden horns,
Flashing his baleful eyes.

(Sunset)

The sun is an eagle old,
There in the windless west.
Atop of the spirit-cliffs
He builds him a crimson nest.

# Metaphor

## The Moon's the North Wind's Cookie by Vachel Lindsay

The moon's the North Wind's cookie.

He bites it, day by day,

Until there's but a rim of scraps

That crumble all away.

The South Wind is a baker.

He kneads clouds in his den,

And bakes a crisp new moon that greedy

North Wind eats again!

## What the Snow Man Said by Vachel Lindsay

The moon's a snowball. See the drifts

Of white that cross the sphere.

The moon's a snowball, melted down

A dozen times a year.

Yet rolled again in hot July

When all my days are done

And cool to greet the weary eye

After the scorching sun.

# Metaphor

## What the Rattlesnake Said by Vachel Lindsey

The moon's a little prairie-dog.

He shivers through the night.

He sits upon his hill and cries

For fear that *I* will bite.

The sun's a broncho. He's afraid

Like every other thing,

And trembles, morning, noon and night,

Lest *I* should spring, and sting.

## The Full Moon by Rowena Bastin Bennet

Out of the clouds,

    all soapy white,

The wind blew a bubble,

    gleaming, bright.

It floated all night,

    in the bowl of the sky

and burst when the rooster

    woke to cry.

# Metaphor

## The Harvest Moon by Lorrie L. Birchall

The harvest moon is big and round,

a pumpkin burning bright;

It watches over empty fields

all through the autumn night.

## Daisies by Frank Dempster Sherman

At evening when I go to bed

I see the stars shine overhead;

They are the little daisies white

That dot the meadow of the Night.

And often while I'm dreaming so,

Across the sky the Moon will go;

It is a lady, sweet and fair,

Who comes to gather daisies there.

For, when at morning I arise,

There's not a star left in the skies;

She's picked them all and dropped them down

Into the meadows of the town.

# Metaphor

## The Night by G. Orr Clark

The night is a big black cat
The moon is her topaz eye,
The stars are the mice she hunts at night,
In the field of the sultry sky.

## Night is a Giant Gardener by Rowena Bastin Bennett

Night is a giant gardener
    Who does his work on high;
His black soil is the darkness,
    His garden is the sky.
The four winds are his shovel,
    The stars, his scattered seeds;
And when the clouds go blowing by
    He's digging up his weeds.
He pulls the moon up by the roots,
    And when his work is done
There blooms one great, big flower
    That people call THE SUN.

# Metaphor

## By Day the Sea by John Richard Moreland

By day the sea
Is a blue flower
With curling white petals,
And the great ships,
Speeding before the wind,
White moths.

## Ship Masts by Evelyn Scott

They stand there
Stark as church spires;
Bare stalks that will blossom—
Tomorrow perhaps—
Into flowers of the wind.

## A Yacht Out at Sea by Ella Wheeler Wilcox

A yacht from its harbor ropes pulled free,
And leaped like a steed o'er the race track blue,
Then up behind her, the dust of the sea.

(Bonus: Can you tell which two poems also have a simile?)

# Metaphor

## The Wasp by William Sharp

Where the ripe pears droop heavily
The yellow wasp hums loud and long
His hot and drowsy autumn song:
A yellow flame he seems to be,
When darting suddenly from high
He lights where fallen peaches lie:
Yellow and black, this tiny thing's
A tiger-soul on elfin wings.

## The Grasshopper by Vachel Lindsay

The grasshopper, the grasshopper,
I will explain to you:
He is the brownies' racehorse,
The fairies' kangaroo.

## The Woodpecker by John B. Tabb

The wizard of the woods is he,
For in his daily round,
Where'er he finds a rotting tree,
He makes the timber sound.

# Metaphor

## Combing and Curling by Gelett Burgess

In the ocean of my hair,

Many little waves are there;

Make the comb, a little boat,

Over all the billows float;

Sail the rough and tangled tide

Till it's smooth on every side,

Till, like other little girls,

I've a sea of wavy curls!

## Mr. Tongue by Unknown

A little red man in a little red house

With gates of ivory!

He *might* stay there, as still as a mouse,

And nobody could see;

But talk he will, and laugh he will,

At everything you do;

And come to the door and peep, until

I know his name—don't you?

# Metaphor

## Thoughts by Hilda Conkling

My thoughts keep going far away
Into another country under a different sky:
My thoughts are sea-foam and sand;
They are apple-petals fluttering.

## Thunderstorms by W.H. Davies

My mind has thunderstorms,
That brood about for heavy hours;
Until they rain me words,
My thoughts are drooping flowers
And sulking, silent birds.

Yet come, dark thunderstorms,
And brood your heavy hours;
For when you rain me words,
My thoughts are dancing flowers
And joyful singing birds.

# Metaphor

## The Coin by Sara Teasdale

Into my heart's treasury
I slipped a coin
That time cannot take
Nor a thief purloin—
Oh better than the minting
Of a gold-crowned king
Is the safe-kept memory
Of a lovely thing.

## Shell Castles by Rowena Bastin Bennet

A sea shell is a castle
Where a million echoes roam,
    A wee castle,
    Sea castle,
Tossed up by the foam;
    A wee creature's,
    Sea creature's,
Long deserted home.

# Metaphor

## Death is a Fisherman by Benjamin Franklin

Death is a fisherman, the world we see
His fish-pond is, and we the fishes be;
His net some general sickness; howe'er he
Is not so kind as other fishers be;
For if they take one of the smaller fry,
They throw him in again, he shall not die:
But Death is sure to kill all he can get,
And all is fish with him that comes to net.

## Brooms by Dorothy Aldis

On stormy days
when the wind is high
tall trees are brooms
sweeping the sky.
They swish their branches
in buckets of rain,
and swash and sweep it
blue again.

# What is Meter?

Meter is the rhythmic pattern of a poem's syllables.

It is decided by the number of syllables in the line,

and how the syllables are **stressed**.

Each rhythm unit is called a **foot**.

(Hint: Sometimes it's easier to identify the meter

if you *overstress* the syllables as you read them aloud.)

## Hickory Dickory Dock -Traditional Nursery Rhyme

**Hickory, dickory, dock,**

/ - -     / - -     /

The **mouse** ran **up** the **clock.**

-     /     -     /     -     /

The **clock** struck **one,**

-     /     -     /

The **mouse** ran **down.**

-     /     -     /

**Hickory, dickory , dock.**

/ - -     / - -     /

# Meter

## Three Blind Mice -Mother Goose Nursery Rhyme

**Three blind mice**,

**See how** they run!

They **all** ran **aft**er the **far**mer's **wife**

She **cut** off their **tails** with a **carving knife**,

Did **ev**er you **see** such a **sight** in your **life**

As **three blind mice**!

# What is Mood & Tone?

**Mood** is the overall feeling of a poem.

**Tone** is the poet's "voice" or attitude toward
the poem or audience

## Mood...

- is the atmosphere of the poem (humorous, serious, sad, creepy)

- is the emotion and feeling it creates *for you as the reader*

- asks: "How does the poem make you *feel?*"

## Tone...

- is the writer's (poet's) attitude toward his/her subject or audience

- helps create *a particular kind of atmosphere or mood*

- is closely related to mood & <u>*voice*</u>

- asks: "In what *tone of voice* should the poem be read
  to effectively convey the right *mood* of the poem?"

# The Joke You Just Told by Unknown

The joke you just told isn't funny one bit.
It's pointless and dull, wholly lacking in wit.
It's so old and stale, it's beginning to smell!
Besides, it's the one I was going to tell.

(The mood is humorously disgruntled and the tone is sarcastic.)

# Mood & Tone

Reading many poems about the same subject
can help understand differences in **mood** and **tone**.

**Subject** is what a poem is generally about.
A poem can be about anything and everything from boats or shoes to abstract things like love or happiness.

**Mood** is the overall feeling the poem creates ***in the reader***.
When you read a poem, does it make you feel content, agitated, frustrated or sad?

**Tone** is more ***a reflection of the writer*** of the poem, rather than the reader.
Tone is the writer's attitude toward the audience. If the poet were to read their poem aloud to you, what tone of "voice" do you imagine they would use?
Would it be sarcastic, somber, objective, amused, angry or friendly?

The author's specific word choice affects the overall mood and tone of a poem. Words can feel positive, negative or neutral. By reading and comparing several poems of the same subject, it becomes somewhat easier to recognize differences in mood & tone.

As you read each poem, ask yourself these questions:

**Mood:** As the reader, how does the poem make me *feel?*
**Tone:** How would I describe the "voice" of the poet author?
(In what *tone of voice* should the poem be read aloud?)

Does the mood or tone ever *change* in a poem?

# Mood & Tone
## Subject: Birds

## A Minor Bird by Robert Frost

I have wished a bird would fly away,

And not sing by my house all day;

Have clapped my hands at him from the door

When it seemed as if I could bear no more.

The fault must partly have been in me.

The bird was not to blame for his key.

And of course there must be something wrong

In wanting to silence any song.

## Be Like the Bird by Victor Hugo

Be like the bird, who

Halting in his flight

On limb too slight

Feels it give way beneath him,

Yet sings

Knowing he hath wings.

# Mood & Tone
## Subject: Birds

## A Bird by Emily Dickinson

A bird came down the walk:

He did not know I saw;

He bit an angleworm in halves

And ate the fellow, raw.


And then he drank a dew

From a convenient grass,

And then hopped sidewise to the wall

To let a beetle pass.

## What Does Little Birdie Say by Alfred Lord Tennyson

What does little birdie say

In her nest at peep of day?

"Let me fly," says little birdie,

"Mother, let me fly away."

"Birdie, rest a little longer,

Till thy little wings are stronger,"

So she rests a little longer,

Then she flies away.

# Mood & Tone
# Subject: Birds

## Once I Saw a Little Bird by Unknown

Once I saw a little bird,
  Come hop, hop, hop;
So I cried, "Little bird,
  Will you stop, stop, stop?"
And was going to the window,
  To say, "How do you do?"
When he shook his little tail,
  And far away he flew.

## Little Birds by Unknown

Little birds sit in their nest and beg,
All mouth that once had been all egg.

# Mood & Tone
## Subject: Birds

## Parrots by Rachel Field

Whenever a parrot looks at me,

I feel all strange and shivery,

For, oh, a parrot's bead-bright eyes

Are keen as wizard's and as wise,

And when they turn and stare at you,

You feel as if they somehow knew

The things you keep all tucked away

Inside yourself and never say.

They stare and shine, and shine and stare,

And you must stand before them there

And feel there's nothing in your mind

A wise old parrot couldn't find.

## The Ostrich is a Silly Bird by Mary E. Wilkins Freeman

The ostrich is a silly bird,

    With scarcely any mind.

He often runs so very fast,

    He leaves himself behind,

And when he gets there, has to stand

    And hang about till night,

Without a blessed thing to do

    until he comes in sight.

# Mood & Tone
# Subject: Spiders

## Daddy Longlegs by Anne L. Huber

A big old daddy longlegs
Creeping on the wall,
I wish that he would go away,
I don't like him at all.

I know he will not hurt me,
But I don't want him here;
So get you gone, old daddy,
And don't come again so near.

## The Itsy Bitsy Spider –Traditional Nursery Rhyme

The itsy bitsy spider crawled up the water spout.
Down came the rain, and washed the spider out.
Out came the sun, and dried up all the rain,
and the itsy bitsy spider went up the spout again.

# Mood & Tone

## Subject: Spiders

# The Spider and the Ghost of a Fly by Vachel Lindsay

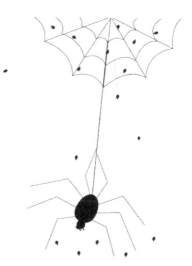

Once I loved a spider
When I was born a fly,
A velvet-footed spider
With a gown of rainbow-dye.

She ate my wings and gloated.
She bound me with a hair.
She drove me to her parlor
Above her winding stair.

To educate young spiders
She took me all apart.
My ghost came back to haunt her.
I saw her eat my heart.

# Mood & Tone
## Subject: Spiders

## Don't Kill the Spider by H.P. Nichols

Don't kill the spider, little Fred,
But come and stand by me,
And watch him spin that slender thread,
Which we can hardly see.

How patiently, now up, now down,
He brings that tiny line!
He never stops, but works right on,
And weaves his web so fine.

You could not make a thread so small,
If you should try all day;
So never hurt him, dear, at all,
But spare him in your play.

# Mood & Tone
## Subject: Spiders

## I'm a Little Spider by Unknown

I'm a little spider,
Watch me spin.
If you'll be my dinner,
I'll let you come in.
Then I'll spin my web
to hold you tight,
and gobble you up
in one big bite!

## Little Miss Muffet -Traditional Nursery Rhyme

Little Miss Muffet
Sat on a tuffet,
Eating her curds and whey;
Along came a spider,
Who sat down beside her
And frightened Miss Muffet away.

# Mood & Tone
# Subject: Dogs

## The Hairy Dog by Herbert Asquith

My dog's so furry I've not seen
His face for years and years;
His eyes are buried out of sight,
I only guess his ears.

When people ask me for his breed,
I do not know or care:
He has the beauty of them all
Hidden beneath his hair.

## I've Got a Dog by Unknown

I've got a dog as thin as a rail,
He's got fleas all over his tail;
Every time his tail goes flop,
The fleas on the bottom all hop to the top.

## His Highness's Dog by Unknown

I am his Highness's dog at Kew;
Pray, tell me sir, whose dog are you?

# Mood & Tone

## Subject: Dogs

## My Father Owns the Butcher Shop by Unknown

My father owns the butcher shop,

My mother cuts the meat,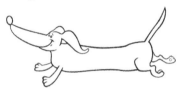

And I'm the little hot dog

That runs around the street.

## There Was a Little Dog by Unknown

There was a little dog, and he had a little tail,

And he used to wag, wag, wag it!

 But when he was sad,

Because he'd been bad,

On the ground he would drag, drag, drag it!

## An Unsaintly Dog by Peter Newell

"My doggie is a Saint Bernard,"

said Bertha small and quaint.

"But he's too ill behaved, I think,

to really be a Saint."

# Mood & Tone
## Subject: Dogs

## The Puppy by Oliver Herford

The Puppy cannot mew or talk,

He has a funny kind of walk,

His tail is difficult to wag

And that's what makes him walk zig-zag.


He is the Kitten of a Dog,

From morn till night he's all agog—

Forever seeking something new

That's good but isn't meant to chew.


He romps about the Tulip bed,

And chews the Flowers white and red,

And when the Gardener comes to see

He's sure to blame mamma or me.


One game that cannot ever fail

To please him is to chase his tail—

(To catch one's tail, 'twixt me and you,

Is not an easy thing to do.)


If he has not a pretty face

The Puppy's heart is in its place.

I'm sorry he must grow into

A Horrid, Noisy Dog, aren't you?

# Mood & Tone
## Subject: Boats & Ships

## Where Go the Boats? By Robert Louis Stevenson

Dark brown is the river,

Golden is the sand.

It flows along forever

With trees on either hand.


Green leaves a-floating,

Castles of the foam,

Boats of mine a-boating—

Where will all come home?


On goes the river

And out past the mill,

Away down the valley,

Away down the hill.


Away down the river,

A hundred miles or more,

Other little children

Shall bring my boats ashore.

# Mood & Tone
## Subject: Boats & Ships

## Ghost Ship by E.R.

Night falls softly on the bay
As the ghost ship sails o'er the bar;
A hero rides upon the deck,
Cold and still as a distant star.

Long years ago a ship sailed out,
Slowly it passed the cheering pack;
Now no one in the town will know
When the ghost ship sails back.

Over the bay the ghost ship sails,
A pale phantom of long ago,
And a hero sails her back again—
But in the town, no one will know.

## The Island by A.A. Milne

If I had a ship,
I'd sail my ship,
I'd sail my ship
Through Eastern seas;
Down to a beach where the slow waves thunder—
The green curls over and the white falls under—
Boom! Boom! Boom!
On the sun-bright sand.

153

# Mood & Tone
## Subject: Boats & Ships

### Romance by Gabriel Setoun

I saw a ship a-sailing,

A-sailing on the sea;

Her masts were of the shining gold,

Her deck of ivory;

And sails of silk, as soft as milk,

And silver shrouds had she.

And round about her sailing,

The sea was sparkling white,

The waves all clapped their hands and sang

To see so fair a sight.

They kissed her twice,

they kissed her thrice,

And murmured with delight.

### My Ship by A.A. Milne

When I am in my ship, I see

The other ships go sailing by.

A sailor leans and calls to me

As his ship goes sailing by.

Across the sea he leans to me,

Above the winds I hear him cry:

*"Is this the way to Round-the-World?"*

He calls as he goes by.

154

# Mood & Tone
## Subject: Cats

## The Lazy Cat by Palmer Cox

There lives a good-for-nothing cat,
so lazy it appears,
that chirping birds can safely come
and light upon her ears.

And rats and mice can venture out
to nibble at her toes,
or climb around and pull her tail,
and boldly scratch her nose.

Fine servants brush her silken coat
and give her cream for tea;
Yet she's a good-for-nothing cat,
as all the world may see.

## Peter and Polly by Unknown

Peter is a funny cat;
His playmate is a cow.
Yet Peter can't say, "Moo!" like that,
And Polly can't say "Meow!!"

155

# Mood & Tone
## Subject: Cats

## The Everlasting Cat by W.B. Rands

I am the cat of cats. I am

The everlasting cat!

Cunning, and old, and sleek as jam,

The everlasting cat!

I hunt vermin in the night—

The everlasting cat!

For I see best without the light-

The everlasting cat!

## There Once Were Two Cats of Kilkenny by Unknown

There once were two cats of Kilkenny,

Each thought there was one cat too many,

    So they fought and they fit,

    And they scratched and they bit,

Till, excepting their nails and the tips of their tails,

Instead of two cats, there weren't any.

156

# Mood & Tone
## Subject: Cats

## Two Little Kittens, One Stormy Night by Unknown

Two little kittens, one stormy night,

Began to quarrel, and then to fight;

One had a mouse and the other had none,

And that's the way the quarrel begun.


"I'll have that mouse," said the biggest cat,

"You'll have that mouse? We'll see about that!"

"I will have that mouse," said the eldest son;

"You shan't have that mouse," said the little one.


I told you before 'twas a stormy night

When these two little kittens began to fight;

The old woman seized her sweeping broom,

And swept the two kittens right out of the room.


The ground was covered with frost and snow,

And the two little kittens had nowhere to go.

So they laid them down on the mat at the door

While the old woman finished sweeping the floor.


Then they crept in, as quiet as mice,

All wet with snow and as cold as ice;

For they found it was better, that stormy night,

To lie down and sleep than to quarrel and fight.

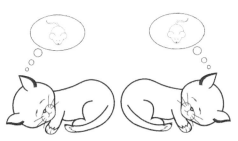

# Mood & Tone
## Subject: Crocodiles

# How Doth the Little Crocodile by Lewis Carroll

How doth the little crocodile

Improve his shining tail,

And pour the waters of the Nile

On every golden scale!


How cheerfully he seems to grin

How neatly spreads his claws,

And welcomes little fishes in,

With gently smiling jaws!

# The Considerate Crocodile by Edwin C. Ranck

There was once a considerate crocodile

Who lay on the banks of the River Nile,

And he swallowed a fish with a face of woe,

While his tears ran fast to the stream below…

"I am mourning," said he, the untimely fate

Of the dear little fish that I just now ate."

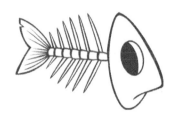

# Mood & Tone

## Subject: Crocodiles

## Mary Had a Crocodile by Unknown

Mary had a crocodile
That ate a child each day;
But interfering people came
And took her pet away.

## If You Should Meet a Crocodile by Unknown

If you should meet a crocodile,
Don't take a stick and poke him;
Ignore the welcome in his smile,
Be careful not to stroke him.

For as he sleeps upon the Nile,
He thinner gets and thinner;
And whene'er you meet a crocodile
He's ready for his dinner.

# Mood & Tone
## Subject: Rainy Weather

## Rain by Robert Louis Stevenson

The rain is raining all around,
It falls on field and tree,
It rains on the umbrellas here,
And on the ships at sea

## The Rainy Day by Henry W. Longfellow

The day is cold, and dark, and dreary;
It rains, and the wind is never weary;
The vine still clings to the mouldering wall,
But at every gust the dead leaves fall,
And the day is dark and dreary!

My life is cold, and dark, and dreary;
It rains, and the wind is never weary;
My thoughts still cling to the mouldering past,
But the hopes of youth fall thick in the blast,
And the days are dark and dreary.

Be still, sad heart, and cease repining;
Behind the clouds is the sun still shining;
Thy fate is the common fate of all,
Into each life some rain must fall,
Some days must be dark and dreary.

# Mood & Tone
## Subject: Rainy Weather

## Rain in Summer by Henry W. Longfellow

How beautiful is the rain!
After the dust and heat,
In the broad and fiery street,
In the narrow lane,
How beautiful is the rain!

How it clatters along the roofs,
Like the tramp of hoofs!
How it gushes and struggles out
From the throat of the overflowing spout!

Across the window pane
It pours and pours;
And swift and wide,
With a muddy tide,
Like a river down the gutter roars
The rain, the welcome rain!

In the country, on every side,
Where far and wide,
Like a leopard's tawny and spotted hide,
Stretches the plain,
To the dry grass and the drier grain
How welcome is the rain!

# Mood & Tone
## Subject: Rainy Weather

## Summer Shower by Emily Dickinson

A Drop fell on the Apple Tree –
Another – on the Roof –
A Half a Dozen kissed the Eaves –
And made the Gables laugh –

A few went out to help the Brook,
That went to help the Sea –
Myself Conjectured were they Pearls –
What Necklaces could be …

## Summer Drizzle by Walter F. Kohn

Stately the silken raindrops fall
like spinnings of some silent spider
into the pool, where sudden small
circles grow wide and wider . . . .

Air is a summer fabric, cool and thin,
Woven of silken threads the raindrops spin.

# Mood & Tone
## Subject: Autumn

## September by Helen Hunt Jackson

The goldenrod is yellow,
the corn is turning brown,
the trees in apple orchards
with fruit are bending down.

By all these lovely tokens
September days are here,
with summer's best of weather
and autumn's best of cheer.

## October by Thomas Bailey Aldrich

October turned my maple's leaves to gold;
The most are gone now;
Here and there one lingers.
Soon these will slip
from out the twig's weak hold,
Like coins between
a dying miser's fingers.

# Mood & Tone
## Subject: Autumn

## The Mist and All by Dixie Willson

I like the fall,

The mist and all.

I like the night owl's

Lonely call—

And wailing sound

Of wind around.


I like the gray

November day,

And bare, dead boughs

That coldly sway

Against my pane.

I like the rain.


I like to sit

And laugh at it—

And tend

My cozy fire a bit.

I like the fall—

The mist and all.

# Mood & Tone
## Subject: Houses

## The Nicest House by Ralph Bergengren

I'd rather live in my house
Than any house I know.
It's got the biggest chimneys.
The roof is long and low.

It's got such funny windows.
Its door is wide and green.
A nicer house than my house
I think was never seen.

Inside it's got a pantry
Of quite the largest size,
Where always there are doughnuts,
And always there are pies.

It's got a lot of book shelves,
A million books, I'm sure;
And those that have the pictures
Are right down near the floor.

Upstairs it's got an attic,
And there I keep my toys.
I'd rather live in my house
Than any other boys.

# Mood & Tone
## Subject: Houses

## The Old House by Walter de la Mare

A very, very old house I know—
And ever so many people go,
Past the small lodge, forlorn and still,
Under the heavy branches, till
Comes the blank wall, and there's the door.
Go in they do; come out no more.
No voice says aught; no spark of light
Across that threshold cheers the sight;
Only the evening star on high
Less lonely makes a lonely sky,
As, one by one, the people go
Into that very old house I know.

## Old Houses by Rachel Field

I think old houses are like Grandmothers,
With lilacs for their purple ribbon bows,
Their upper windows square as spectacles;
And most of all a look—as if they watched
The road for someone, gone so long ago
That only they remember who it was
And why they wait there patiently all day.

166

# Mood & Tone
## Subject: Houses

## In a Dark, Dark Wood by Unknown

In a dark, dark wood,

There was a dark, dark house.

And in that dark, dark house,

There was a dark, dark room.

And in that dark, dark room,

There was a dark, dark cupboard.

And in that dark, dark cupboard,

There was a dark, dark shelf.

And on that dark, dark shelf,

There was a dark, dark box.

And in that dark, dark box,

There was a GHOST!

## Song for a Little House by Christopher Morley

I'm glad our house is a little house,

Not too tall nor too wide;

I'm glad the hovering butterflies

Feel free to come inside.


Our little house is a friendly house,

It is not shy or vain;

It gossips with the talking trees,

And makes friends with the rain.

# What is a Narrative Poem?

A narrative poem is a story poem, so it tends to be a longer poem.

It has at least one character and a plot with a beginning, middle & end.

Sometimes, it has a conflict & resolution.

## The Three Little Kittens –Traditional Nursery Rhyme

Three little kittens they lost their mittens,

And they began to cry,

Oh, mother dear, we sadly fear

Our mittens we have lost.

What! Lost your mittens, you naughty kittens!

Then you shall have no pie.

Meow, meow, meow.

No, you shall have no pie.

The three little kittens they found their mittens,

And they began to cry,

Oh, Mother dear, see here, see here,

Our mittens we have found!

Put on your mittens, you silly kittens,

And you shall have some pie.

Purr, purr, purr,

Oh, let us have some pie.

The three little kittens put on their mittens,

And soon ate up the pie;

Oh, Mother dear, we greatly fear

Our mittens we have soiled.

What! Soiled your mittens, you naughty kittens!

Then they began to sigh,

Meow, meow, meow.

Then they began to sigh.


The three little kittens they washed their mittens,

And hung them out to dry;

Oh! Mother dear, do you not hear,

Our mittens we have washed!

What! Washed your mittens, you good little kittens,

But I smell a rat close by.

Meow, meow, meow.

We smell a rat close by.

# Narrative Poem

## Old Mother Hubbard -Traditional Nursery Rhyme

Old Mother Hubbard
Went to the cupboard
To get her poor dog a bone;
But when she got there,
The cupboard was bare,
And so the poor dog had none.

She went to the baker's
To buy him some bread;
And when she came back,
The poor dog was dead.

She went to the joiner's
To buy him a coffin;
And when she came back,
The doggy was laughin'.

She went to the butcher's
To buy him some tripe;
And when she came back,
He was smoking his pipe.

She went to the hatter's
To buy him a hat;
And when she came back,
He was feeding the cat.

She went to the barber's
To buy him a wig;
And when she came back,
He was dancing a jig.

She went to the tailor's
To buy him a coat;
And when she came back,
He was riding a goat.

She went to the cobbler's
To buy him some shoes;
And when she came back,
He was reading the news.

# Narrative Poem

## The Three Billy Goats Gruff by Clara Doty Bates

Three billy goats, by the name of Gruff,

Thinking themselves not fat enough,

And looking out for a place for sweet

Young grass grew plenty for them to eat,

Saw, over the river, a sunny knoll;

      But the bridge was long,

      And the stream was strong,

And under the bridge lived an ugly Troll.

This Troll was a wicked, long nosed elf,

Who owned the whole of the bridge himself.

And when the smallest billy goat, Gruff—

His poor little coat all shabby and rough—

Started to cross, with hoofs tip-tap,

The bridge gave the Troll a sign "Trip, trap!"

And the troll called out, with a surly frown;

      "Who's that tripping,

      Who's that skipping

Over my bridge? I'll gobble him down!

      I'll gobble him down!"

"'Tis I, the tiniest billy-goat Gruff!

      Oh, don't eat me! Oh, don't eat me!

For I'm very little and lean and tough.

Wait for the other,

Wait till my brother,

The second billy-goat Gruff goes by.

He's larger and plumper far than I!"

"Run on," said the Troll, "I'll see!"


By and by the second old billy-goat Gruff,

With his coat of shaggy, long haired stuff,

Stepped with his hoofs on the bridge, tip-tap,

And the bridge gave the sign again, "Trip-Trap!"

And the Troll called out with an ugly frown;

"Who's that tripping,

Who's that skipping

Over my bridge? I'll gobble him down!

I'll gobble him down!"


"'Tis I, the second big billy-goat Gruff,

Scarcely the half of a pound in weight

If my shaggy long-haired coat was off!

Wait for the other,

Wait till my brother,

The third big billy-goat Gruff goes by;

He's bigger and fatter far than I!"

"Pass on!" said the Troll, "I'll wait!"


By and by the great, big billy-goat Gruff

Stalked on the bridge, all burly and bluff;

It creaked and groaned, and bent with a snap,

And gave the sign, "Trip-Trap! Trip-Trap!"

And the Troll roared out with an awful frown;

"Who's that blundering,

Who's that thundering

Over my bridge? I'll gobble him down!

I'll gobble him down!"

"'Tis I, the great big billy-goat Gruff,

Come out from under the bridge and see!"

And his voice was heavy and hoarse and rough—

"I am the other,

I am that brother,

The biggest and fattest of all three!"

Then on his horns all crooked and bare,

And long, he tossed the Troll in the air,

So high that he never came down again.

And after that,

All grew so fat,

With eating the young grass on the hill,

That, if they have not grown lean since then,

They're all of them fat still.

# Narrative Poem

## Goldilocks & the Three Bears by Walter Crane

Some time ago, ere we were born or thought of,

There lived a little girl, who liked to roam

Through lonely woods and lanes, unknown, unsought of

Such folk who like to stop and stay at home.


She found out curious things in all her travel

And one of her adventures I will tell:

Once, in a wood she saw a path of gravel,

Which led to a small cottage in a dell.


And, as the door stood open, in walked boldly,

This child, whose name was Goldilocks, I'm told;

There was nobody there to treat her coldly,

No friend to call her back, no nurse to scold.


She found herself within a parlor charming;

And there upon the table there were placed

Three basins, sending up a smell so warming,

That she at once felt hungry, and must taste.

The largest basin first, but hot and biting
The soup was in it, and the second too;
The smallest basin tasted so inviting,
That up she ate it all, with small ado.

And next she saw three chairs, and tried to sit in
The biggest, but it was too hard and high;
The middle one she scarcely seemed to fit in,
But in the smallest chair sat easily;

And rocked herself, her ease and comfort taking,
Singing the pretty songs she knew so well;
When, oh! The little chair cracked loud, and, breaking,
Gave way all suddenly, and down she fell.

"Ah, well," she thought, "there may be beds to lie on
Upstairs; I think I'll go at once and see."
And so there were; she said aloud, "I'll try one,
For I am tired and sleepy as can be."

The biggest bed was not of feathers, surely,
It was so hard; and so she tried the next,
And found it little better; but securely
She slept upon the smallest one, unvext.

The little house belonged to bears, not persons;
The Father Bear, so very rough and large;
The Mother Bear (I have known many worse ones);
And then the little Cub, their only charge.

They had gone for a walk before their dinner;

Returning, Father growled, "Who's touched my soup?"

"Who's touched my soup?" said Mother, with voice thinner;

"But mine," said little Cub, "is finished up!"


They turned to draw their chairs a little nearer;

"Who's sat in my chair?" growled the Father Bear;

"Who's sat in my chair?" said the Mother, clearer;

And squeaked the little Cub, "Who's broken my small chair?"


They rushed upstairs, and Father Bruin, growling,

Cried out, "Who's lain upon my bed?"

"Who's lain on mine?" cried Mother Bruin, howling;

"But someone lies on mine!" the small Bear said.


"We'll kill the child, and eat her for our dinner,"

The Father growled; but said the Mother, "No;

For supper she shall be, and I will skin her."

"No," said the little Cub, "we'll let her go."


So Goldilocks, in sudden terror flying,

Reached home; and when the Nurse the story hears,

She says, "You are in luck, there's no denying,

To get away in safety from THREE BEARS."

# Narrative Poem

## The Little Red Hen by Unknown

Once, a mouse, a frog, and a little red hen
    Together kept a house;
The frog was the laziest of frogs,
    And lazier still was the mouse.

The work all fell on the little red hen,
    Who had to get all the wood,
And build the fires, and scrub, and cook,
    And sometimes hunt the food.

One day, as she went scratching round,
    She found a bag of rye,
Said she, "Now who will make some bread?"
    Said the lazy mouse, "Not I."

"Nor I," croaked the frog as he drowsed in the shade,
    Red hen made no reply,
But flew around with bowl and spoon,
    And mixed and stirred the rye.

Who'll make the fire to make the bread?"
    Said the mouse again, "Not I,"
And scarcely opening sleepy eyes,
    Frog made the same reply.

The little red hen said never a word,

But a roaring fire she made.

And while the bread was baking brown,

"Who'll set the table?" she said.


"Not I," said the sleepy frog with a yawn;

"Nor I," said the mouse again,

So the table she set, and the bread put on,

"Who'll eat this bread?" said the hen.


"I will," cried the frog. "And I," squeaked the mouse,

As they near the table drew:

"Oh, no you won't!" said the little red hen,

And away with the loaf she flew!

# Narrative Poem

## The Princess That Wasn't by Oliver Herford

In a very lonely tower,
So the legend goes to tell,
Pines a princess in the power
Of a dreadful dragon's spell.
There she sits in silent state,
Always watching—always glum,
While the dragon at the gate

Eats her suitors as they come—
King and prince of every nation
Poet, page, and troubadour,
Of whatever rank or station—
Eats them up and waits for more.

Every knight that hears the legend
Thinks he'll see what he can do,
Gives his sword a lovely edge, and—
Like the rest is eaten too!
All of which is very pretty,
And romantic, too, forsooth;
But, somehow, it seems a pity
That they shouldn't know the truth.
If they only knew that really
There is no princess to gain—
That she's an invention merely

180

Of the crafty dragon's brain.

Once it chanced he'd missed his dinner

For perhaps a day or two;

Felt that he was getting thinner,

Wondered what he'd better do.

Then it was that he bethought him

How in this romantic age

(Reading fairy tales had taught him)

Rescuing ladies was the rage.

So a lonely tower he rented,

For a trifling sum per year,

And this thrilling tale invented,

Which was carried far and near.


Far and near throughout the nations,

And the dragon ever since,

Has relied for daily rations,

On some fearless knight or prince.

And while his romantic fiction

To a chivalrous age appeals,

It's a very safe prediction:

He will never want for meals.

# Classic Narrative Poems Turned Picture Books

Narrative poems tell a complete story with a beginning, middle & end,
so it's no wonder some talented illustrators have turned these
classic narrative poems into beautifully illustrated picture books.

## The Spider and the Fly by Mary Howitt

The narrative poem, written by Mary Howitt in 1829,
became a 2003 Caldecott Honor award-winning picture book
by illustrator Tony diTerlizzi.

## Over in the Meadow by Olive A. Wadsworth

Since 1870, this narrative poem has been a very popular
counting rhyme by Olive A. Wadsworth. Several picture
book versions have been published by numerous publishers.
This example was illustrated by the very talented Ezra Jack
Keats.

## The Owl and the Pussycat by Edward Lear

This nonsense narrative poem was first published in 1871 by
Edward Lear and there are several picture book versions. This
one features pictures by the highly acclaimed illustrator Jan
Brett.

# Classic Narrative Poems Turned Picture Books

## Casey at the Bat by Ernest L. Thayer

First published in the San Francisco Examiner on June 3, 1888, this classic narrative poem celebrates the all American sport of baseball. This picture book edition is illustrated by Jim Hull.

## Over the River and Through the Wood

by Lydia Maria Child

Written in 1844, this Thanksgiving classic has been turned into picture books and also a popular holiday song. This picture book example is illustrated by Christopher Manson.

## 'Twas the Night Before Christmas by

Clement C. Moore

First published in 1823, "A Visit From St. Nicholas," or "'Twas the Night Before Christmas," is perhaps the best-known narrative poem…ever. Several picture book versions have been published, but this beautiful classic is illustrated by Charles Santore.

Also note: There are many wonderful contemporary picture books and chapter books written completely in verse.

# What is Near Rhyme?

Near rhymes are *close* to a full rhyme…but just not quite.

Near rhymes are also called
half-rhymes, slant rhymes, approximate rhymes, or imperfect rhymes.

Examples:

soul/all

coast/lost

muffin/stuffing

Poets and songwriters use near rhyme…

- to increase the word choice available

- to surprise the reader with something unexpected

- to add tension because it is a little jarring

One of the most famous poets to use slant (near) rhyme was
Emily Dickinson, an American poet (1830-1886).

## Hope by Emily Dickinson

Hope is the thing with feathers
That perches in the **soul**,
And sings the tune without the words,
And never stops at **all**.

# Near Rhyme

## A Little Boat by Emily Dickinson

'Twas such a little, little boat
That toddled down the bay!
'Twas such a gallant, gallant sea
That beckoned it away!
'Twas such a greedy, greedy wave
That licked it from the coast:
Nor ever guessed the stately sails
My little craft was lost!

## As to the Weather by Unknown

I remember, I remember,

    As my childhood flitted by,

It was cold then in December,

    And was warmer in July.

In the winter there were freezings—

    In the summer there were thaws;

But the weather isn't now at all

    Like what it used to was!

# Near Rhyme

## The Old Person of Sparta by Edward Lear

There was an old person of Sparta,
Who had twenty-five sons and one daughter;
    He fed them on snails,
    And weighed them in scales,
That wonderful person of Sparta.

## The Old Man of Calcutta by Edward Lear

There was an old man of Calcutta,
Who perpetually ate bread and butter;
    Till a great bit of muffin,
    On which he was stuffing,
Choked that old man of Calcutta.

## The Young Lady of Portugal by Edward Lear

There was a young lady of Portugal,
Whose ideas were excessively nautical;
    She climbed up a tree
    to examine the sea,
But declared she would never leave Portugal.

# Near Rhyme

## Baa, Baa, Black Sheep -Traditional Nursery Rhyme

Baa, baa, black sheep,
Have you any wool?
Yes, sir, yes, sir,
Three bags full;

One for my master,
One for my dame,
And one for the little boy
Who lives down the lane.

## Little Tommy Tittlemouse -Traditional Nursery Rhyme

Little Tommy Tittlemouse
Lived in a little house;
He caught fishes
In other men's ditches.

## The Sea by Unknown

Behold the wonders of the mighty deep,
Where crabs and lobsters learn to creep,
And little fishes learn to swim,
And clumsy sailors tumble in.

# What is a Nonsense Poem?

A nonsense poem often doesn't make a lot of sense.

It simply plays with language and is meant to be fun.

Many nursery rhymes are nonsense poems.

## Hey, Diddle, Diddle! -Traditional Nursery Rhyme

Hey, diddle, diddle!

The cat and the fiddle,

The cow jumped over the moon;

The little dog laughed

To see such a sport,

And the dish ran away with the spoon.

## Bat, Bat -Traditional Nursery Rhyme

Bat, bat,

Come under my hat,

And I'll give you a slice of bacon;

And when I bake

I'll give you a cake

If I am not mistaken.

# Nonsense Poem

## The Flying Pig -Traditional Nursery Rhyme

Dickory, dickory, dare,

The pig flew up in the air;

The man in brown soon brought him down,

Dickory, dickory, dare.

## Duckle, Duckle, Daisy by LeRoy F. Jackson

Duckle, duckle, daisy,

Martha must be crazy,

She went and made a Christmas cake

Of olive oil and gluten-flake,

And set it in the sink to bake,

Duckle, duckle, daisy.

## Six Little Salmon by LeRoy F. Jackson

I sing a funny song from away out west,

Of six little salmon with their hats on;

How they all left home—but I forget the rest—

The six little salmon with their hats on.

189

# Nonsense Poem

## A Beetle by LeRoy F. Jackson

A beetle once sat on a barberry twig,
And turned at the crank of a thingamajig.
Needles for hornets, nippers for ants,
For the bumblebee baby a new pair of pants,
For the grizzled old gopher a hat and a wig,
The beetle ground out of his thingamajig.

## On the Road to Tattletown by LeRoy F. Jackson

On the road to Tattletown
What is this I see?
A pig upon a pedestal,
A cabbage up a tree,
A rabbit cutting capers
With a twenty dollar bill—
Now if I don't get to Tattletown
Then no one ever will.

# Nonsense Poem

## The Jumblies by Edward Lear

They went to sea in a Sieve, they did,

In a Sieve they went to sea:

In spite of all their friends could say,

On a winter's morn, on a stormy day,

    In a Sieve they went to sea!


And when the Sieve turned round and round,

And every one cried, "You'll all be drowned!"

They called aloud, "Our Sieve ain't big,

But we don't care a button! We don't care a fig!

    In a Sieve we'll go to sea!"


Far and few, far and few,

Are the lands where the Jumblies live;

Their heads are green, and their hands are blue,

    And they went to sea in a Sieve.

# Nonsense Poem

## Two Old Kings by Carolyn Wells

Oh! The King of Kanoodledum

And the King of Kanoodledee,

   They went to sea

   In a jigamaree—

A full-rigged jigamaree.

And one king couldn't steer,

And the other, no more could he;

   So they both upset

   And they both got wet,

As wet as wet could be.

## Order in the Court by Unknown

Order in the court

The judge is eating beans

His wife is in the bathtub

Shooting submarines.

# Nonsense Poem

## The Queen of Nonsense Land by Carolyn Wells

This is the Queen of Nonsense Land,

She wears her bonnet on her hand;

She carpets her ceilings and frescos her floors,

She eats on her windows and sleeps on her doors.

Oh, ho! Oh, ho! To think there could be

A lady so silly-down-dilly as she!

She goes for a walk on an ocean wave,

She fishes for cats in a coral cave;

She drinks from an empty glass of milk,

And lines her potato trees with silk.

I'm sure that fornever and never was seen

So foolish a thing as the Nonsense Queen!

She ordered a wig for a blue bottle fly,

And she wrote a note to a pumpkin pie;

She makes all the oysters wear emerald rings,

And does dozens of other nonsensible things.

Oh! The scatterbrained, shatterbrained lady so grand,

Her Royal Skyhighness of Nonsense Land!

# What is Onomatopoeia?

(pronounced on-uh-mat-uh-**pee**-uh)

Onomatopoeic words appeal to the five senses
and imitate the *sounds* of the words they refer to.

Examples:

- clang
- whoosh
- beep
- plop
- buzz
- roar

# Toot! Toot! by Unknown

A peanut sat on a railroad track,

His heart was all a-flutter;

The five fifteen came rushing by

**Toot! Toot!**  Peanut butter!

## Static by Gertrude Van Winkle

Hear that **crinkly, crackly** static

Perhaps it's fairies in the attic.

# Onomatopoeia

## Wild Beasts by Evaleen Stein

I will be a lion

And you shall be a bear,

And each of us will have a den

Beneath a nursery chair;

And you must growl and growl and growl,

I will roar and roar,

And then—why then—you'll growl again,

And I will roar some more!

## The Old Lady of France by Edward Lear

There was an old lady of France,

Who taught little ducklings to dance;

    When she said, "Tick-a-tack!"

    They only said, "Quack!"

Which grieved that old lady of France.

# Onomatopoeia

## Hipperty, Clickerty, Clackerty, Bang by LeRoy F. Jackson

Hipperty, clickerty, clackerty, bang,

Get in a corner as fast as you can!

The sideboard is tipsy, the table is mad,

The chairs have lost all the sense that they had.

So hipperty, clickerty, clackerty, bang,

Get in a corner as fast as you can!

## Through the Jungle the Elephant Goes by Unknown

Through the jungle the elephant goes,

Swaying his trunk to and fro,

Munching, crunching, tearing trees,

Stamping seeds, eating leaves.

His eyes are small, his feet are fat,

Hey, elephant, don't do that!

# Onomatopoeia

## Buzz, Buzz, Buzz by Clara Doty Bates

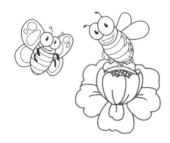

"Buzz, Buzz, Buzz,"—says the great buzzing bee,

"Go away butterfly, this flower is for me."

"Why? Why? Why?" says the little butterfly,

"If you may sit on this flower, why mayn't I?"

## The Bashful Earthquake by Oliver Herford

The Earthquake rumbled

And mumbled

And grumbled;

And then he bumped,

And everything tumbled—

Bumpety-thump!

Thumpety-bump!—

Houses and palaces all in a lump!

"Oh, what a crash!

Oh, what a smash!

How could I ever be so rash?"

The Earthquake cried.

# Onomatopoeia

## Time by Unknown

The watch is ticking, ticking,
Ticking the minutes away;
And minutes make up the hours,
And hours make up the day.

The clock is striking, striking,
The hours so loud and clear;
The hours make up the day,
And the days make up the year.

## Oom-Pah by Hugh Lofting

Oom-pah, boom-pah, oom-pah boom!

Like roses soon our cheeks will bloom.

We only ask for elbow-room

Oom-pah, boom-pah, oom-pah boom!

# Onomatopoeia

## The Squirrel by Unknown

Whisky, frisky,
Hippity hop;
Up he goes
To the tree top!

Whirly, twirly,
Round and round,
Down he scampers
To the ground.

Furly, curly
What a tail!
Tall as a feather
Broad as a sail!

Where's his supper?
In the shell,
Snappity, crackity,
Out it fell.

# Onomatopoeia

## The Farmer and the Raven -Traditional Nursery Rhyme

A farmer went trotting upon his gray mare,

    Bumpety, bumpety, bump!

With his daughter behind him so rosy and fair,

    Lumpety, lumpety, lump!

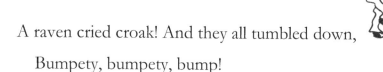

A raven cried croak! And they all tumbled down,

    Bumpety, bumpety, bump!

The mare broke her knees, and the farmer his crown,

    Lumpety, lumpety, lump!

The mischievous raven flew laughing away,

    Bumpety, bumpety, bump!

And vowed he would serve them the same the next day,

    Lumpety, lumpety lump!

## "Croak!" Said the Toad -Old Garden Rhyme

"Croak!" said the toad. "I'm hungry, I think.

Today I've had nothing to eat or to drink.

I'll crawl to a garden and jump through the pales,

And there I'll dine nicely on slugs and on snails."

# Onomatopoeia

## Old Granny Cricket's Rocking Chair by Clara Doty Bates

Old Granny Cricket's rocking-chair,

Creakety-creak, creakety-creak!—

Back and forth, and here and there,

Squeakety-squeak, squeakety-squeak!—


On the hearth-stone, every night,

Rocks and rocks in the cheery light.

Little old woman, dressed in black,

With spindling arms and a crooked back.

She sits with a cap on her wise old head,

And her eyes are fixed on the embers red;

She does not sing, she does not speak,

But the rocking-chair goes creakety-creak!


## The Frog of Lake Okeefinokee by Laura E. Richards

There once was a frog,

And he lived in a bog,

On the banks of Lake Okeefinokee.

And the words of the song

That he sang all day long

Were, "Croakety croakety croaky."

# Onomatopoeia

## The Shower by Unknown

Hear the rain, patter, patter,

On the pane, clatter, clatter!

Down it pours, helter, pelter;

Quick indoors! Shelter! Shelter!

See it gush, and roar and whirl,

Swiftly rush, eddy and swirl

Through the street and down the gutters!

How it splashes—but we don't care

Though it dashes everywhere.

We don't care, for peeping through—

See! Up there—a patch of blue!

And the sun, in spite of rain,

Has begun to smile again.

## A Farmyard Talk by Unknown

The big brown hen and Mrs. Duck

Went walking out together;

They talked about all sorts of things—

The farmyard, and the weather.

But all I heard was:

"Cluck! Cluck! Cluck!"

And "Quack! Quack! Quack!"

From Mrs. Duck.

# What is Parody?

Parody is the imitation of another's work
usually in a humorous way.
It's important to be familiar with the original work
to understand the parody.

Parody…

- imitates another person's work

- is meant to be funny by poking fun

- sometimes becomes even more popular than the original

In 1898, poet Gelett Burgess published a nonsense poem titled, "The Purple Cow." The poem became so well-known, it was often *parodied* by other poets.

## The Purple Cow by Gelett Burgess

I never saw a purple cow,
I never hope to see one;
But I can tell you, anyhow,
I'd rather see than be one.

# Parody

## To Gelett Burgess by Edwin C. Ranck

I never saw a purple cow,
You say you never saw one;
But this I'll tell you anyhow,
I know that I can draw one.

## I've Never Seen a Purple Cow by Unknown

I've never seen a purple cow.
My eyes with tears are full.
I've never seen a purple cow,
And I'm a purple bull.

Eventually, Gelett Burgess even parodied his *own poem*.

## Confession by Gelett Burgess

Ah, yes, I wrote "The Purple Cow"—
I'm sorry, now, I wrote it;
But I can tell you anyhow
I'll kill you if you quote it.

Gelett Burgess
(1866-1951)

# Parody

In 1885, Robert Louis Stevenson, author of *Treasure Island* and *Strange Case of Dr. Jekyll and Mr. Hyde*, wrote a children's poetry anthology titled, *A Child's Garden of Verses*. It was an instant success and many of his poems are often included in children's poetry anthologies today.

Robert Louis Stevenson

(1850-1894)

**A Child's Garden of Verses**

First published in 1885

In 1911, twenty-six years later, writer and illustrator Oliver Herford wrote *The Kitten's Garden of Verses*, a (cat version) parody of *A Garden of Verses*. Herford's poems can stand completely on their own, but the reader will find them more humorous and understand the parody if already familiar with Stevenson's original poems.

Oliver Herford

(1860-1904)

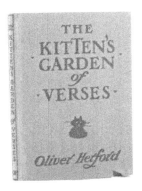

**The Kitten's Garden of Verses**

Published in 1911

# Parody

## My Shadow by Robert Louis Stevenson

I have a little shadow that goes in and out with me,
And what can be the use of him is more than I can see.
He is very, very like me, from the heels up to the head;
And I see him jump before me, when I jump into my bed.

The funniest thing about him is the way he likes to grow—
Not at all like proper children, which is always very slow;
For he sometimes shoots up taller, like an India-rubber ball,
And he sometimes gets so little that there's none of him at all.

## The Shadow Kitten by Oliver Herford

There's a funny little kitten that tries to look like me,
But though I'm round and fluffy, he's as flat as flat can be;
And when I try to mew to him he never makes a sound,
And when I jump into the air he never leaves the ground.

He has a way of growing, I don't understand at all.
Sometimes he's very little and sometimes he's very tall.
And once when in the garden when the sun came up at dawn
He grew so big I think he stretched half-way across the lawn.

# Parody

## Happy Thought by Robert Louis Stevenson

The world is so full of a number of things,

I'm sure we should all be as happy as kings.

## Happy Thought by Oliver Herford

The world is so full of a number of Mice

I'm sure that we all should be happy and nice.

## Rain by Robert Louis Stevenson

The rain is raining all around,

It falls on field and tree,

It rains on the umbrellas here,

And on the ships at sea.

## Rain by Oliver Herford

The rain is raining everywhere,

Kittens to shelter fly—

But Human Folk wear overshoes,

To keep their hind paws dry.

# Parody

## Bed in Summer by Robert Louis Stevenson

In winter I get up at night
And dress by yellow candle-light.
In summer, quite the other way,
I have to go to bed by day.

I have to go to bed and see
The birds still hopping on the tree,
Or hear the grown-up people's feet
Still going past me in the street.

And does it not seem hard to you,
When all the sky is clear and blue,
And I should like so much to play,
To have to go to bed by day?

# Parody

## Winter and Summer by Oliver Herford

In Winter when the air is chill,

And winds are blowing loud and shrill,

All snug and warm I sit and purr,

Wrapped in my overcoat of fur.

In Summer quite the other way,

I find it very hot all day,

But Human People do not care,

For they have nice thin clothes to wear.

And does it not seem hard to you,

When all the world is like a stew,

And I am much too warm to purr,

I have to wear my Winter Fur?

.

# Parody Mash-Up

Poets of the 19th and early 20th century really liked to parody each other's poems.

In *The Re-Echo Club* by Carolyn Wells, the following poem cleverly parodies **both** the Robert Louis Stevenson poem, "Bed in Summer," and the Gelett Burgess poem, "The Purple Cow."

## The Purple Cow: If Written by Robert Louis Stevenson

by Carolyn Wells

In winter I get up at night

And hunt that cow by lantern light;

In summer quite the other way,

I seek a purple cow by day.

And does it not seem strange to you,

I can't find cows of purple hue?

But, I can tell you, anyhow,

I'm glad I'm not a purple cow.

# Parody Mash-Up

Original poem:

## There Was a Little Girl by Henry Wadsworth Longfellow

There was a little girl,

Who had a little curl,

Right in the middle of her forehead.

When she was good,

She was very, very good,

But when she was bad, she was horrid.

Parody of the original poem:

## There Was a Little Girl: If Written by Robert Louis Stevenson by Carolyn Wells

In winter, I go up at night

And curl that curl by candlelight;

In summer, quite the other way,

I have to curl it twice a day.

When I am good, I seem to be

As good as peaches on the tree;

But when I'm bad I've awful ways,

I'm horrid, everybody says.

And does it not seem hard to you,

I have to choose between the two?

When I'm not happy, good and glad,

I have to be so awful bad.

# Parody

Sometimes poets parody well-known nursery rhymes.

Original Nursery Rhyme:

## Mary Had a Little Lamb by Sarah Josepha Hale

Mary had a little lamb,

It's fleece was white as snow,

And everywhere that Mary went,

The lamb was sure to go.

Parody of "Mary Had a Little Lamb"

## Brutal Mary by Edwin C. Ranck

Mary had a little lamb,

The lamb was always buttin.'

So Mary killed the little lamb

And turned him into mutton.

# Parody

Original Nursery Rhyme:

## Twinkle, Twinkle, Little Star by Jane Taylor

Twinkle, twinkle, little star,
How I wonder what you are!
Up above the world so high,
Like a diamond in the sky.

Parody of "Twinkle, Twinkle, Little Star"

## Twinkle, Twinkle, Little Bat by Lewis Carroll

Twinkle, twinkle, little bat!
How I wonder what you're at!
Up above the world you fly,
Like a tea-tray in the sky!

# What is Personification?

Personification is giving non-humans (objects, animals, concepts)
human qualities and characteristics.

Personification...

- uses very human **adjectives, verbs,** and **adverbs** to describe non-humans

- brings a poem to life by connecting with human feelings

- helps a poet connect emotionally with their audience

- helps create vivid imagery

- is often part of a larger metaphor

Example:

The <u>wind</u> ***stood up*** and ***gave a shout.***

# The Wind Stood Up by James Stephens

The wind stood up and gave a shout;
He whistled on his fingers, and
Kicked the withered leaves about
And thumped the branches with his hand,
And said he'd kill, and kill, and kill,
And so he will, and so he will.

# Personification

## The Wind by Abbie Farwell Brown

The Wind comes stealing o'er the grass

To whisper pretty things;

And though I cannot see him pass,

I feel his careful wings.

## Birch Trees by John Richard Moreland

The night is white,

The moon is high,

The birch trees lean

Against the sky.

The cruel winds

Have blown away

Each little leaf

Of silver gray.

O lonely trees

As white as wool . . .

That moonlight makes

So beautiful

# Personification

## Fog by Carl Sandburg

The fog comes
on little cat feet.
It sits looking
over harbor and city
on silent haunches
and then moves on.

## The Sun and Fog Contested by Emily Dickinson

The Sun and the Fog contested
The Government of the Day—
The Sun took down his yellow whip
And drove the Fog away.

## A Weather Game by Anna M. Pratt

The sun and rain in fickle weather
Were playing hide and seek together,
And each in turn would try to chase
The other from his hiding place.
At last they met to say goodbye,
And so a rainbow spanned the sky.

# Personification

## The White Window by James Stephens

The moon comes every night to peep
Through the window where I lie,
And I pretend to be asleep;
But I watch the moon as it goes by,
And it never makes a sound.

It stands and stares, and then it goes
To the house that's next to me,
Stealing on its tippy-toes,
To peep at folk asleep maybe;
And it never makes a sound.

## Duty by Edwin Markham

When Duty comes a-knocking at your gate,
Welcome him in; for if you bid him wait,
He will depart only to come once more
And bring seven other duties to your door.

# Personification

## The Unseen by Sara Teasdale

Death went up the hall
Unseen by every one,
Trailing twilight robes
Past the nurse and the nun.

He paused at every door
And listened to the breath
Of those who did not know
How near they were to Death.

Death went up the hall
Unseen by nurse and nun;
He passed by many a door
But he entered one.

## Look Back on Time by Emily Dickinson

Look back on Time with kindly eyes,
He doubtless did his best;
How softly sinks his trembling sun
In human nature's west!

# Personification

## The Night by James Stephens

The Night was creeping on the ground!
She crept, and did not make a sound

Until she reached the tree: And then
She covered it, and stole again

Along the grass beside the wall!
I heard the rustling of her shawl

As she threw blackness everywhere
Along the sky, the ground, the air,

And in the room where I was hid!
But, no matter what she did

To everything that was without,
She could not put my candle out!

So I stared at the Night! And she
Stared back solemnly at me!

# Personification

## Sleep by Rowena Bastin Bennett

Sleep walks in at the door
    And she neither speaks nor sings,
But her breath is sweeter than song
    And folded are her wings;
And the children play no more
When sleep walks in at the door.

## Racing the Train by Rowena Bastin Bennett

I race him down the platform,

The puffing, snorting train.

He takes so long at starting

That it's not hard to gain

At first, but when his steam is up

He's haughty as can be;

He chuckles hoarsely to himself

Because he's passing me.

# Personification

## Laughter by John Kendrick Bangs

Worry stalked along the road,

Trouble sneaking after;

Then Black Care, and Grief, and Goad

Enemies to Laughter.


But old Laughter with a shout

Rose up and attacked 'em;

Put the sorry pack to rout,

Walloped 'em and whacked 'em.


Laughter frivols day and night;

Sometimes he's a bubble,

But he hath a deal of might

In a bout with Trouble!

## Early by Dorothy Aldis

I was up so tip toe early

That the flowers were all pearly

As they waited in their places

For the sun to dry their faces.

# Personification

## September by Ethel Romig Fuller

Lilies still lift

Their laughter to the sun,

Fishes carve the air

And waves still run

On glad, bare feet

Along the pebbly shore,

Lapping the wharf

And the boathouse door.

But nightwinds chant

Sagas of grief,

And the lake holds

A yellow leaf.

## Strings in the Earth by James Joyce

There's music along the river

For Love wanders there,

Pale flowers on his mantle,

Dark leaves on his hair.

# Personification

## October's Party by George Cooper

October gave a party;
The leaves by hundreds came—
The Chestnuts, Oaks, and Maples,
And leaves of every name.
The Sunshine spread a carpet,
And everything was grand,
Miss Weather led the dancing,
Professor Wind the band.

## Ice by Charles G.D. Roberts

When Winter scourged the meadow and the hill
And in the withered leafage worked his will,
The water shrank, and shuddered, and stood still—
Then built himself a magic house of glass,
Irised with memories of flowers and grass,
Wherin to sit and watch the fury pass.

# Personification

## The Wind Giant by Rowena Bastin Bennett

The March Wind strides in seven league boots
    Across the snow patched mountain-sides;
Adown the ice-bound river chutes
    The March wind strides.

Beneath a magic cloak he hides
    His giant form, and as he scoots,
The helter-skelter rain he guides.

He tramples on the tingling roots,
    His head the scurrying cloud divides.
As in his mighty, seven league boots,
    The March Wind Strides.

## April by Kenneth M. Ellis

She came and stood upon the threshold;
A smile about her visage played,
And stern March laughed—his chill breath froze her—
And April wept—she was afraid!

224

# Personification

## The Old Bridge by Hilda Conkling

The old bridge has a wrinkled face.

He bends his back

For us to go over.

He moans and weeps

But we do not hear.

Sorrow stands in his face

For the heavy weight and worry

Of people passing.


The trees drop their leaves into the water;

The sky nods to him.

The leaves float down like small ships

On the blue surface

Which is the sky.

He is not always sad:

He smiles to see the ships go down

And the little children

Playing on the river banks.

# What is Point of View?

A poem is usually expressed from someone's

(or something's) point of view.

A poem may have more than one perspective.

A poem may be written in:

- **first person**    (I, we)
- **second person**   (you)
- **third person**    (he, she, it, they)

Example: (First Person—I)

## Anticipation by Oliver Herford

When **I** grow up **I** mean to be
A lion large and fierce to see.
**I'll** mew so loud that Cook in fright
Will give **me** all the cream in sight.

And anyone who dares to say
"Poor Thing" to **me** will rue the day.
Then having swallowed him **I'll** creep
Into the guest room bed to sleep.

# Point of View: First Person Perspective

## I'm Glad the Sky is Painted Blue by Unknown

I'm glad the sky is painted blue,
    And the earth is painted green,
With such a lot of nice fresh air
    All sandwiched in between.

## My Size by LeRoy F. Jackson

I'm much too big for a fairy,
And much too small for a man,
    But this is true:
    Whatever I do,
I do it the best I can.

## August Heat by Unknown

In August, when the days are hot,
I like to find a shady spot
And hardly move a single bit—
    And sit—

      And sit—
        And sit—
          And sit!

227

# Point of View: First Person Perspective

## Gold by Laura E. Richards

In the earth's dark bosom

Long I slumbered deep,

Till the hardy miners

Woke me from my sleep.

Now I flash and glitter,

Now I'm bought and sold,

Everyone for me does run,

For my name is Gold.

## My Dream -Brave Buffalo, Sioux

When I was but a child

I dreamed a wondrous dream.

I went upon a mountain;

There I fell asleep. I heard a voice say,

"Now will I appear to you."

A buffalo said this to me, dreaming.

When I was but a child

I dreamed this wondrous dream.

# Point of View: First Person Perspective

## Theme in Yellow by Carl Sandburg

I spot the hills

With yellow balls in autumn.

I light the prairie cornfields

Orange and tawny gold clusters

And I am called pumpkins.

On the last of October

When dusk is fallen

Children join hands

And circle round me

Singing ghost songs

And love to the harvest moon;

I am a jack-o'-lantern

With terrible teeth

And the children know

I am fooling.

## When I Become a Werewolf by Lorrie L. Birchall

When I become a werewolf,

I serenade the moon,

but no one likes my howling,

because I'm out of tune.

# Point of View: First Person Perspective

## The Magic Vine by Unknown

A fairy seed I planted,

so dry and white and old.

There sprang a vine enchanted

with magic buds of gold.


I watched it, I tended it,

and as the days went by,

it grew a Jack o' lantern

and a great Thanksgiving pie!

## Turkey Time by Unknown

Thanksgiving Day will soon be here;

It comes around but once a year.

If I could only have my way,

We'd have Thanksgiving every day!

# Point of View: First Person Perspective

## The Wind by Unknown

I am the wind
And I come very fast.
Through the tall wood
I blow a loud blast.

Sometimes I am soft
As a sweet, gentle child,
I play with the flowers,
Am quiet and mild,

And then out so loud
All at once I can roar.
If you wish to be quiet
Close window and door.

I am the wind
And I come very fast,
Through the tall wood
I blow a loud blast.

# Point of View: First Person Perspective

## The March Wind by Unknown

I come to work as well as play;
    I'll tell you what I do;
I whistle all the live-long day,
    "Woo-oo-oo-oo! Woo-oo!"

I toss the branches up and down
    And shake them to and fro,
I whirl the leaves in flocks of brown,
    And send them high and low.

I strew the twigs upon the ground,
    The frozen earth I sweep;
I blow the children round and round
    And wake the flowers from sleep.

## Beyond Winter by Ralph Waldo Emerson

Over the winter glaciers
I see the summer glow.
And through the wild-piled snowdrift
The warm rosebuds below.

# Point of View: First Person Perspective

## The Cowboy by Unknown

All day long on the prairies I ride,
Not even a dog to trot by my side;
My fire I kindle with chips gathered round,
My coffee I boil without being ground.

I wash in a pool and wipe on a sack;
I carry my wardrobe all on my back;
For want of an oven I cook bread in a pot,
And sleep on the ground for want of a cot.

My ceiling is the sky, my floor is the grass,
My music is the lowing of the herds as they pass;
My books are the brooks, my sermons the stones,
My parson is a wolf on his pulpit of bones.

## A Bridge by Gelett Burgess

I'd never dare to walk across
A bridge I cannot see,
For quite afraid of falling off
I fear that I should be!

# Point of View: First Person Perspective

## The Road Not Taken by Robert Frost

Two roads diverged in a yellow wood,

And sorry I could not travel both

And be one traveler, long I stood

And looked down one as far as I could

To where it bent in the undergrowth;

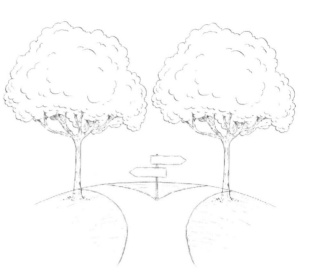

Then took the other, as just as fair,

And having perhaps the better claim,

Because it was grassy and wanted wear;

Though as for that the passing there

Had worn them really about the same,

And both that morning equally lay

In leaves no step had trodden black.

Oh, I kept the first for another day!

Yet knowing how way leads on to way,

I doubted if I should ever come back.

I shall be telling this with a sigh

Somewhere ages and ages hence:

Two roads diverged in a wood, and I—

I took the one less traveled by,

And that has made all the difference.

# Point of View: Second Person Perspective

## Bedtime by Gelett Burgess

The night is different from the day—
It's darker in the night;
How can you ever hope to play
When it's no longer light?

When bedtime comes, it's time for you
To stop, for when you're yawning,
You should be dreaming what you'll do
When it's tomorrow morning.

## Whoever You Are by Unknown

Whoever you are, be noble;
Whatever you do, do well;
Whenever you speak, speak kindly,
Give joy wherever you dwell.

# Point of View: Second Person Perspective

## Winter Wise -Traditional Rhyme

Walk fast in snow, in frost walk slow,
And still as you go tread on your toe;
When frost and snow are both together,
Sit by the fire, and spare shoe leather.

## The Squirrel by John B. Tabb

Who combs you, little squirrel?
And do you twist and twirl
When someone puts the rollers on
To keep your tail in curl?

And must you see the dentist
For every tooth you break?
And are you apt from eating nuts
To get a stomachache?

# Point of View: Second Person Perspective

## Borrowing by Gelett Burgess

Whose doll is that on the table?

    Whose book is that on the chair?

The knife and the pencils and other utensils,

    Now how do they come to be there?

Didn't you say they were borrowed?

    You'd better take back just a few!

If *you* lent your playthings, I think you would say things

    If no one returned them to you!

## Carnivore Teeth by Lorrie L Birchall

You had sharp teeth for tearing meat,

from dinosaurs you planned to eat.

# Point of View: Second Person Perspective

## Fireflies by Carolyn Hall

Little lamps of the dusk
You fly low and gold
When the summer evening
Starts to unfold.
So that all the insects,
Now, before you pass,
Will have light to see by
Undressing in the grass.

But when night has flowered,
Little lamps agleam,
You fly over tree-tops
Following a dream.
Men wonder from their windows
That a firefly goes so far.
They do not know your longing
To be a shooting star.

238

# Point of View: Third Person Perspective

## The Lion by Oliver Herford

The lion does not move at all,
Winter, summer, spring or fall,
He does not even stretch or yawn,
But lies in silence on the lawn.

## The Giraffe by Oliver Herford

He rises at the break of day,
And starts his breakfast right away.
His food has such a way to go—
His throat's so very long and so—
An early breakfast he must munch
To get it down in time for lunch.

## The Elephant by Hilaire Belloc

When people call this beast to mind,
They marvel more and more
At such a little tail behind,
So large a trunk before.

# Point of View: Third Person Perspective

## A Farmer's Boy by Unknown

They strolled down the lane together,

The sky was studded with stars—

They reached the gate in silence

And he lifted down the bars—

She neither smiled nor thanked him

Because she knew not how;

For he was just a farmer's boy

And she was a jersey cow.

## Tow Truck by R.A Stevens

Up the road, and down the road,

The busy tow truck goes

To start a stubborn car that's stalled,

Or pull one from the snows.

It is a bright, important red,

And very smart it feels,

When it comes back with someone's car

A-tagging at its heels!

# Point of View: Third Person Perspective

## The Ostrich by Elizabeth Gordan

Ostrich grows to be immense
But has so very little sense,
For when an enemy's at hand
He covers up his head with sand.

## The Runner by Walt Whitman

On a flat road runs the well trained runner,
He is lean and sinewy with muscular legs,
He is thinly clothed, he leans forward as he runs,
With lightly closed fists and arms partially raised.

## A Wise Old Owl by Unknown

A wise old owl sat in an oak,
The more he heard, the less he spoke;
The less he spoke, the more he heard;
Why aren't we all like that wise old bird?

# Point of View: Third Person Perspective

## The Woodpecker by Elizabeth Madox Roberts

The woodpecker pecked out a little round hole
And made him a house in the telephone pole.
One day in the winter, he poked out his head,
And he had on a hood and a collar of red.

When the streams of rain pour out of the sky,
And the sparkles of lightning go flashing by,
And the big, big wheels of thunder roll,
He can snuggle back in the telephone pole.

## Peacocks by Rose Fyleman

Peacocks sweep the fairies' rooms;
They use their folded tails for brooms;
But fairy dust is brighter far
Than any mortal colors are;

And all about their tails it clings
In strange designs of rounds and rings;
And that is why they strut about
And proudly spread their feathers out.

# What is a Pun?

A pun plays on the *multiple meanings* and *spellings* of some words.

- Some words, called *homonyms*, have the same spelling, but different meanings.

  Example:    nut— something to eat

  nut— a goofy person

## Don't Worry if Your Job is Small by Unknown

Don't worry if your job is small
And your rewards are few.
Remember that the mighty oak,
Was once a nut like you.

- Some words, called *homophones*, sound alike, but are spelled differently & have different meanings.

  Example:    Time—units of seconds, minutes, hours, days…

  Thyme— a leafy herb

## The Flower School by Abbie Farwell Brown

The flowers study in their beds,
And all recite in rhyme.
The lesson first put in their heads
Is how to tell the Thyme.

# Puns

## Have You Ever Seen? by Unknown

Have you ever seen a sheet on a river bed?

Or a single hair from a hammer's head?

Has the foot of a mountain any toes?

And is there a pair of garden hose?


Does the needle ever wink its eye?

Why doesn't the wing of a building fly?

Can you tickle the ribs of a parasol?

Or open the trunk of a tree at all?


Are the teeth of a rake ever going to bite?

Have the hands of a clock any left or right?

Can the garden plot be deep and dark?

And what is the sound of the birch's bark?

## Seasons by Unknown

There was a young fellow named Hall,

Who fell in the spring in the fall;

    'Twould have been a sad thing

    If he'd died in the spring,

But he didn't —he died in the fall.

# Puns

## Elephant by Unknown

The elephant carries a great big trunk;
He never packs it with clothes;
It has no lock and it has no key
But he takes it wherever he goes.

## Raising Frogs for Profit by Unknown

Raising frogs for profit
is a very sorry joke.
*How* can you make money
when so many of them croak?

## A Lament by John B. Tabb

"O Lady Cloud, why are you weeping?" I said.
"Because," she made answer, "my rain-beau is dead."

245

# Puns

## The Sun by Gelett Burgess

The sun is low, to say the least,

Although it is well-red;

Yet, since it rises in the yeast,

It should be better bred!

## Do You Carrot All for Me? by Unknown

Do you carrot all for me?

My heart beets for you,

With your turnip nose

And your radish face,

You are a peach.

If we cantaloupe,

Lettuce marry:

Weed make a swell pear.

# What is a Refrain?

A refrain is a **repeated phrase or line** in a poem.

A poem may have more than one refrain,

and sometimes it can change in the poem.

A refrain is used…

- for emphasis and importance

- for creative effect

- to enhance the rhythm of the poem

Example:

In this poem, the refrain is the poetry line *Higglety, pigglety, pop!*

# Higglety, Pigglety, Pop! by Samuel Goodrich

**Higglety, pigglety, pop!**
The dog has eaten the mop;
The pig's in a hurry,
The cat's in a flurry,
**Higglety, pigglety, pop!**

# Refrain

## Get a Transfer by Unknown

If you are on the Gloomy Line,

Get a transfer.

If you're inclined to fret and pine,

Get a transfer.

Get off the track of doubt and gloom,

Get on the Sunshine Track—there's room—

Get a transfer.


If you're on the Worry Train,

Get a transfer.

You must not stay there and complain,

Get a transfer.

The Cheerful Cars are passing through,

And there's lots of room for you—

Get a transfer.


If you're on the Grouchy Track,

Get a transfer.

Just take a Happy Special back,

Get a transfer.

Jump on the train and pull the rope,

That lands you at the station of Hope—

Get a transfer.

# Refrain

## I Heard a Bird Sing by Oliver Herford

I heard a bird sing

In the dark of December

A magical thing

And sweet to remember.

"We are nearer to Spring

Than we were in September,"

I heard a bird sing

In the dark of December.

## Who Has Seen the Wind? by Christina Georgina Rossetti

Who has seen the wind?

Neither I nor you;

But when the leaves hang trembling

The wind is passing through.

Who has seen the wind?

Neither you nor I;

But when the trees bow down their heads

The wind is passing by.

# Refrain

## Everybody Says by Dorothy Aldis

Everybody says

I look just like my mother.

Everybody says

I'm the image of Aunt Bee.

Everybody says

My nose is like my father's,

But *I* want to look like *me*.

## Teddy Bear, Teddy Bear by Unknown

Teddy Bear, Teddy Bear,

Go upstairs.

Teddy Bear, Teddy Bear,

Say your prayers.

Teddy Bear, Teddy Bear,

Turn out the light.

Teddy Bear, Teddy Bear,

Say good night.

# Refrain

## A Silly Old Octopus by Ruth McEnery Stuart & Albert Bigelow Paine

A silly old octopus lived in the sea,

With a hey-diddle hi-diddle dum;

And the funniest sort of fellow was he,

This silly old octopus under the sea,

With a mouth where the top of his head ought to be,

To swallow the divers that come—

This silly old octopus under the sea,

With a hey-diddle hi-diddle dum.

## Mary Jane by A.A. Milne

*What* is the matter with Mary Jane?

She's crying with all her might and main.

And she won't eat her dinner—rice pudding again—

What *is* the matter with Mary Jane?

*What* is the matter with Mary Jane?

She's perfectly well, and she hasn't a pain;

But, look at her, now she's beginning again!—

What *is* the matter with Mary Jane?

# Refrain

## The Cupboard by Walter de la Mare

I know a little cupboard,

With a teeny tiny key,

And there's a jar of lollipops

For me, me, me.


It has a little shelf, my dear,

As dark as dark can be,

And there's a dish of Banbury cakes

For me, me, me.


I have a small fat grandmamma,

With a very slippery knee,

And she's the keeper of the cupboard

With the key, key, key.

And I'm very good, my dear,

As good as good can be,

There's Banbury cakes, and lollipops

For me, me, me.

# Refrain

## The Lighthouse by Rachel Field

I'd like to be a lighthouse
All scrubbed and painted white.
I'd like to be a lighthouse
And stay awake all night
To keep my eye on everything
That sails my patch of sea;
I'd like to be a lighthouse
With the ships all watching me.

## Buffalo Dusk by Carl Sandburg

The buffaloes are gone.

And those who saw the buffaloes are gone.

Those who saw the buffaloes by thousands and

    how they pawed the prairie sod into dust with their hoofs, their great heads

    down pawing on in a great pageant of dusk,

Those who saw the buffaloes are gone.

And the buffaloes are gone.

# What is Repetition?

Repetition is *anything repeated* such as a:

- sound
- syllable
- word
- phrase
- line
- stanza
- pattern

Whatever is repeated is *emphasized*, making it more important.
Repetition is used to create a:

- mood
- rhythm
- creative effect

Example:

In the following poem, the word *noise* is repeated three times
for emphasis.

## The Saddest Noise by Emily Dickinson

The saddest noise, the sweetest noise,
The maddest noise that grows—
The birds, they make it in the spring,
At night's delicious close.

# Repetition

## The Four Winds by Margaret Sangster

The wind of the West
I love it best.
The wind of the East
I love it least.

The wind of the South
Has sweet in its mouth.
The wind of the North
Sends great storms forth.

## There Was a Crooked Man -Traditional Nursery Rhyme

There was a crooked man, and he went a crooked mile,
He found a crooked sixpence beside a crooked stile;
He bought a crooked cat, which caught a crooked mouse,
And they all lived together in a little crooked house.

# Repetition

## Water by LeRoy F. Jackson

There's water in the rain barrel,
And water in the well,
There's lots of water in the pond
Where Hannah Hawkins fell.

There's water in the ocean,
And water in the skies,
And when a fellow blubbers
He gets water in his eyes.

But in the Barca desert
Where the hippodoodles play,
The water in the rivers
Just dries up and blows away.

## The Wonderful World by W.B. Rands

Great, wide, beautiful, wonderful World,
With the wonderful water round you curled,
And the wonderful grass upon your breast,
World, you are beautifully dressed.

# Repetition

## Happy the Ocean by Unknown

Angry the ocean
In hurricane season

Peaceful the ocean
Its whitecaps napping

Gloomy the ocean
As sky mirrors darken

Sunny the ocean
Yacht riggings snapping

Blue-green the ocean
In deep-shallow waters

Moody the ocean
Gone mad in a minute

Busy the ocean
With cargo and cruises

Happy the ocean
With dolphins in it

# Repetition

## Little by Little by Unknown

"Little by little," an acorn said,
As it slowly sank in its mossy bed.
"I am improving every day,
Hidden deep in the earth away."

Little by little, it sipped the dew;
Little by little, each day it grew;
Downward it sent out a threadlike root,
Up in the air sprung a tiny shoot.

Day after day, and year after year,
Little by little the leaves appear;
And the slender branches spread far and wide,
Till the mighty oak is the forest's pride.

## Weather by Ford Madox Ford

Sometimes wind and sometimes rain,
Then the sun comes back again;
Sometimes rain and sometimes snow,
Goodness, how we'd like to know
Why the weather changes so.

# Repetition

## The Farmer by L. H. Bailey

I hoe and I plow
I plow and I hoe
And the wind drives over the main.

I mow and I plant
I plant and I mow
While the sun burns hot on the plain.

I sow and I reap
I reap and I sow
And I gather the wind with the grain.

I go and I come
I come and I go
In the calm and the storm and the rain.

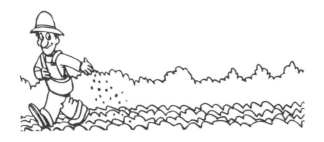

# Repetition

## Something New by Laura E. Richards

There's a new thing at our house:
It's not a cat; it's not a mouse;
It's not a bird; it's not a dog;
It's not a monkey or a frog;
A sweeter thing than any other;
It is my little Baby Brother!

## James James by A.A. Milne

James James
Morrison Morrison
Weatherby George Dupree
Took great
Care of his Mother,
Though he was only three.

James James
Said to his Mother,
*"Mother,"* he said, said he:
*"You must never go down*
*To the end of town,*
*If you don't go down with me."*

# What is Rhyme?

Words with the same **_ending sound_** rhyme.

This is also called **perfect rhyme**.

Examples of rhyming words:

> fish/dish
>
> said/bed
>
> loud/crowd
>
> sleigh/tray

Example:

In this poem, the ending rhymes are _glows/shows_ and _sun/done_.

# The Robin's Bath by Evaleen Stein

A flash and flicker of dripping wings,

A wet red breast that **glows**

Bright as the newly opened bud

The first red poppy **shows**,

A sparkle of flying rainbow drops,

A glint of golden **sun**

On ruffled feathers, a snatch of song,

And the robin's bath is **done**.

# What is a Rhyme Scheme?

**A rhyme scheme** is a **pattern of rhyme**
between lines of a poem.

- Alphabet letters are used to show which lines **rhyme**.
  Lines with the same letter rhyme with each other.

- Since rhyme schemes are a pattern of rhyme, some are simple,
  while others can get very complicated.

- Here are some simple rhyme schemes:

  Monorhyme (AAAA)

  Alternate Rhyme (ABAB)

  Couplet (AA, BB, CC)

  Tercet (AAA, AAB, ABA, ABB, ABC)

  Haiku (ABC)

  Simple 4-Line (ABCB)

  Limerick (AABBA)

# Rhyme Scheme: Monorhyme Scheme

In the **monorhyme scheme,** all of the lines in the poem have the same ending rhyme. (Hint: mono means *one*)

Monorhyme Scheme: **AAAA**

| | |
|---|---|
| street | **A** |
| feet | **A** |
| repeat | **A** |
| beet | **A** |

## A Wonderful Feat by Edwin C. Ranck

I never walk along the **street**
Because I haven't any **feet**;
Nor is this strange when I **repeat**
That I am but a garden **beet**.

## March by Celia Thaxter

Oh March that blusters, and March that **blows**,
what color under your footstep **grows**?
Beauty you summon from winter's **snows**
and you are the pathway that leads to the **rose**.

# Rhyme Scheme: Monorhyme Scheme

## Matilda, Queen of Spain by John Drinkwater

Matilda, who was Queen of Spain,
decreed that no one should complain
if, when they sent her all their rain,
she had it all sent back again.

## Poe at Halloween by Lorrie L. Birchall

Mister Edgar Allan Poe,
wrote some famous verses—so,
at Halloween, you all should know,
I am a raven, not a crow.

## We Are Trick-or-Treaters by Lorrie L. Birchall

Halloween is when we meet,
wearing costumes on the street.
We will ask for something sweet,
when we come to trick-or-treat!

# Rhyme Scheme: Alternate Rhyme

In the **alternate rhyme scheme,** the alternating lines rhyme.

The first and third lines rhyme, and the second and fourth lines rhyme.

Alternate Rhyme Scheme: **ABAB**

honey/funny **A**

life/knife **B**

# I Eat My Peas with Honey by Unknown

| | |
|---|---|
| I eat my peas with **honey**; | **A** |
| I've done it all my <u>life</u>. | **B** |
| It makes the peas taste **funny**, | **A** |
| But it keeps them on the <u>knife</u>. | **B** |

# Encouraged by Paul Laurence Dunbar

| | |
|---|---|
| Because you love me I have much **achieved**, | **A** |
| Had you despised me then I might have <u>failed</u>, | **B** |
| But since I knew you trusted and **believed**, | **A** |
| I could not disappoint you and so <u>prevailed</u>. | **B** |

# Rhyme Scheme: Alternate Rhyme

## The Tale of Taddy Pole

by Ruth McEnery Stuart and Albert Bigelow Paine

There was a little Polliwog—
His name was Taddy Pole.
He lived within a little bog,
beside a crawfish hole.

And all the day did Taddy play
around a sunken log,
until he lost his tail one day,
and then he was a frog.

## An Insectarian by John B. Tabb

"I cannot wash my dog," she said,
"Nor touch him with a comb,
For fear the fleas upon him bred
May find no other home."

## The Polar Bear by Hilaire Belloc

The Polar Bear is unaware
Of cold that cuts me through:
Because he has a coat of hair—
I wish I had one too!

## Neither Out Far Nor in Deep by Robert Frost

The people along the sand
All turn and look one way.
They turn their back on the land.
They look at the sea all day.

As long as it takes to pass
A ship keeps raising its hull;
The wetter ground like glass
Reflects a standing gull.

The land may vary more;
But wherever the truth may be,
The water comes ashore,
And the people look at the sea.

They cannot look out far.
They cannot look in deep.
But when was that ever a bar
To any watch they keep?

# Rhyme Scheme: Alternate Rhyme

## Don't Give Up! by Phoebe Cary

If you've tried and have not won,

Never stop for crying;

All that's great and good is done

Just by patient trying.

If by easy work you beat,

Who the more will prize you?

Gaining victory from defeat,

That's the test that tries you.

## Two Chickens by Ruth McEnery Stuart & Albert Bigelow Paine

Two chickens long debated

On a costume for a ball,

And became so much elated

That they didn't go at all.

# Rhyme Scheme: Alternate Rhyme

## By Special Delivery by John Kendrick Bangs

When I've a quarrel in my mind
With one who's far away,
To scorching letters I'm inclined,
In which I say my say.

And then I take those seething screeds
So full of ink and ire,
In which I threaten awful deeds,
And mail them in the fire!

## Silence by Paul Laurence Dunbar

'Tis better to sit here beside the sea,
Here on the spray-kissed beach,
In silence, that between such friends as we
Is full of deepest speech.

# Rhyme Scheme: Couplet

A rhyming couplet (like a happy couple)
has two lines that rhyme and complete one thought.

The two lines often have the same meter (same stressed syllables).

**AA,** but usually occurs as **AA BB CC DD ...**

## Bashfulness by Robert Herrick

Of all our parts, the eyes **express**    **A**
The sweetest kind of **bashfulness**.    **A**

## Cloud Pictures by Unknown

Among the grass I love to **lie**,    **A**
And watch the fleecy clouds pass **by**:    **A**
For many pictures there I <u>see</u>,    **B**
So clear although so far from <u>me</u>.    **B**

## The Irony of Ants by Lorrie L. Birchall

**Ant**arctica is one location,
the ants don't go for their vacation.

# Rhyme Scheme: Couplet

## A Big Turtle by Unknown

A big turtle sat on the end of a log,

Watching a tadpole turn into a frog.

## A Kite by Unknown

I often sit and wish that I

Could be a kite up in the sky,

And ride upon the breeze and go

Whichever way I chanced to blow.

## I Asked My Mother by Unknown

I asked my mother for fifty cents

To see the elephant jump the fence.

He jumped so high that he touched the sky

And never came back till the Fourth of July.

# Rhyme Scheme: Couplet

## The Little Man Who Wasn't There by Hughes Mearns

Last night I saw upon the stair
a little man who wasn't there.
He wasn't there again today;
Oh, how I *wish* he'd go away!

## Extinction by Lorrie L. Birchall

It's a rather sad distinction,
to be famous for extinction.

## As I Was Going Out by Unknown

As I was going out one day
My head fell off and rolled away.
But when I saw that it was gone,
I picked it up and put it on.

And when I got into the street,
A fellow cried, "Look at your feet!"
I looked at them and sadly said,
"I've left them both asleep in bed!"

# Rhyme Scheme: Couplet

## Witch Broth by Ruth McEnery Stuart & Albert Bigelow Paine

Witches, witches in a tree,
Brew your broth of mystery.
Snail and toad and lizard in it—
Tail of cat and tongue of linnet,
Rabbit's foot and wing of bee—
Witches, witches, none for me.

## White Fields by James Stephens

In the winter children go
Walking in the fields of snow
Where there is no grass at all,
And the top of every wall,
Every fence, and every tree
Is as white as white can be.

Pointing out the way they came,
(Every one of them the same)
All across the fields there be
Prints in silver filigree;
And their mothers find them so
By the footprints in the snow.

# Rhyme Scheme: Couplet

## The Sour Old Lady by Mary Mapes Dodge

There was an old lady all dressed in silk,
Who lived upon lemons and buttermilk;
And, thinking this world was a sour old place,
She carried its acid all over her face.

## The Scarecrow by Annie Stone

Here is the scarecrow, see him stand
Upon the newly planted land;
A figure rugged and forlorn,
A silent watcher of the corn.

His dangling legs, his arms spread wide,
A lone man of the countryside;
Uncouth, the butt of pen and tongue,
Unheralded, unsought, unsung.

To you, old scarecrow, then this lay
To cheer you on your lonely way;
Would that all men, their whole lives through,
Served some good purpose, same as you.

# Rhyme Scheme: Couplet

## The Worm by Ralph Bergengren

When the earth is turned in spring
The worms are fat as anything.

And birds come flying all around
To eat the worms right off the ground.

They like worms just as much as I
Like bread and milk and apple pie.

And once, when I was very young,
I put a worm right on my tongue.

I didn't like the taste a bit,
And so I didn't swallow it.

But oh, it makes my Mother squirm
Because she *thinks* I ate that worm!

## A Lesson from a Sundial by Unknown

Ignore dull days, forget the showers—
Keep count of only shining hours.

# Rhyme Scheme:  Couplet

## The Tired Caterpillar by Unknown

A tired caterpillar went to sleep one day
In a snug little cradle of silken gray.
And he said, as he softly curled up in his nest,
"Oh, crawling was pleasant, but rest is best."

He slept through the winter long and cold,
All tightly up in his blanket rolled,
And at last he awoke on a warm spring day
To find that winter had gone away.

He awoke to find he had golden wings,
And no longer need crawl over sticks and things.
"Oh, the earth is nice," said the glad butterfly,
"But the sky is best, when we learn to fly!"

## An Old Guitar by Ruth McEnery & Albert Bigelow Paine

An old guitar once broke its strings,
And all the musical notes took wings;
They harried away to lands afar.
But two of them stayed with the old guitar.

# Rhyme Scheme: Couplet

## As I Looked Out by Unknown

As I looked out on Saturday last
A fat little pig went hurrying past.
Over his shoulder he wore a shawl,
Although he didn't seem cold at all.

I waved at him, but he didn't see,

For he never so much as looked at me.

Once again, when the moon was high,

I saw the little pig hurrying by.


Back he came at a terrible pace,

The moonlight shone on his little pink face,

And he smiled with a smile that was quite content,

But I never knew where that little pig went.


## Spinning Top by Frank Dempster Sherman

When I spin round without a stop

And keep my balance like the top,

I find that soon the floor will swim

Before my eyes; and then, like him,

I lie all dizzy on the floor

Until I feel like spinning more.

# Rhyme Scheme: Couplet

## Teddy Bear by A.A. Milne

A bear, however hard he tries,
Grows tubby without exercise.

Our Teddy Bear is short and fat,
Which isn't to be wondered at.

But do you think it worries him
To know that he is far from slim?

No, just the other way about—
He's *proud* of being short and stout.

## Somebody by Unknown

Somebody loves you deep and true.
If I weren't so bashful, I'd tell you who.

# Rhyme Scheme: Couplet

## A Thought by Oliver Herford

It's very nice to think of how
In every country lives a cow
To furnish milk with all her might
For kittens' comfort and delight.

## The Grasshopper and the Elephant by Unknown

Way down south where bananas grow,
A grasshopper stepped on an elephant's toe.
The elephant said with tears in his eyes,
"Pick on somebody your own size."

## The Penguin by Elizabeth Gordon

Said Penguin pensively one day:
"Come, fishie dear, come out and play."
But fishie answered back in a fright:
"I've heard about your appetite."

279

# Rhyme Scheme: Couplet

## The Shark by Lord Alfred Douglas

A treacherous monster is the shark
He never makes the least remark.
And when he sees you on the sand,
He doesn't seem to want to land.

He watches you take off your clothes,
And not the least excitement shows.
His eyes do not grow bright or roll,
He has astonishing self-control.

He waits till you are quite undressed,
And seems to take no interest.
And when towards the sea you leap,
He looks as if he were asleep.

But when you once get in his range,
His whole demeanor seems to change.
He throws his body right about,
And his true character comes out.

It's no use crying or appealing,
He seems to lose all decent feeling.
After this warning you will wish
To keep clear of this treacherous fish.

# Rhyme Scheme: Tercet

A **Tercet** has three lines that go together.

In a **tercet**, the rhyme scheme can vary:

- None of the three lines may rhyme (like a haiku ABC)

- All three lines may rhyme in a monorhyme (AAA)

- Any two out of the three lines may rhyme (ABA, AAB, ABB)

## The Lily Princess by Unknown

| | |
|---|---|
| Down from her dainty head | **A** |
| The Lily Princess lightly drops | **B** |
| A spider's airy thread. | **A** |

## Algy Met a Bear by Unknown

| | |
|---|---|
| Algy met a bear, | **A** |
| The bear was bulgy, | **B** |
| The bulge was Algy. | **C** |

# Rhyme Scheme: Tercet

## The Eagle by Alfred, Lord Tennyson

He clasps the crag with crooked hands;
Close to the sun in lonely lands,
Ringed with the azure world, he stands.

The wrinkled sea beneath him crawls;
He watches from his mountain walls,
And like a thunderbolt he falls.

## Firefly by Elizabeth Madox Roberts

A little light is going by,
Is going up to see the sky,
A little light with wings.

I never could have thought of it,
To have a little bug all lit
And made to go on wings.

# Rhyme Scheme: Tercet

## The Little Brown Owl by Clara Doty Bates

The little brown owl sits up in the tree,
And if you look well
His big eyes you may see.

He says whit-a-whoo, when the night grows dark,
And he hears the dogs
and the little foxes bark.

## Snowy Owl Haiku by Unknown

 Listen…in the woods
a snowy owl is eating
the wind's syllable

## Fair Night by Amy Lowell

The chirping of crickets in the night
Is intermittent,
Like the twinkling of stars.

# Rhyme Scheme: Tercet

## The Puncture by Oliver Herford

When I was just a Kitten small,
They gave to me a Rubber Ball
To roll upon the floor.

One day I tapped it with my paw
And pierced the rubber with my claw;
Now it will roll no more.

## A Tortoise by Lorrie L. Birchall

Because he is so very slow,
a tortoise always likes to know,
which direction he should go.

## Rules for Happiness by Immanuel Kant

Something to do,
Something to love,
Something to hope for.

# Rhyme Scheme: Tercet

## The Roaring Frost by Alice Thompson Meynell

A flock of winds came winging from the North,
Strong birds with fighting pinions driving forth
With a resounding call!

Where will they close their wings and cease their cries—
Between what warming seas and conquering skies—
And fold, and fall?

## Shadows of the Ships by Carl Sandburg

Rocking on the crest
In the low blue luster,
Are the shadows of the ships.

## Writing by Amy Lowell

We will scatter little words
Upon the paper
Like seeds about to be planted.

# Rhyme Scheme: Tercet

## The Lost Balloon by Evaleen Stein

Oh dear! My purple toy balloon
Has flown away! And very soon
It will be high up as the moon!

And don't you think the man up there
Will wonder what it is, and stare?
Perhaps he'll say, "*Well, I declare!*"

Or, maybe if it chance there are
Some little boys in yonder star,
And if it floats away so far,

Perhaps they'll jump up very high
And catch the cord as it goes by!
At any rate I hope they'll try!

## The People by Elizabeth Madox Roberts

The ants are walking under the ground,
And the pigeons are flying over the steeple,
And in between are the people.

# Rhyme Scheme: Tercet

## The Pancake by Christina Georgina Rossetti

Mix a pancake,

Stir a pancake,

Pop it in the pan!

Fry the pancake,

Toss the pancake,

Catch it if you can!

## At the Seaside by Robert Louis Stevenson

When I was down beside the sea

A wooden spade they gave to me

To dig the sandy shore.

My holes were empty like a cup.

In every hole the sea came up,

Till it could come no more.

# Rhyme Scheme: Haiku

Haiku (pronounced hī-**koo**) is a form of short Japanese poetry
with three lines that do not rhyme (ABC).
It is often about a nature subject.


**Haiku...**

- usually does *not* have a title

- does not rhyme

- is a tercet because it has three lines

- has seventeen syllables in total

    5 syllables in the first & third lines
    7 syllables in the second line


One fallen flower
Returning to the branch? . . . No!
A white butterfly.

-Moritake


Standing still at dusk
Listen...in far distances
The song of froglings!

-Buson

# Rhyme Scheme: Haiku

Black cloudbank broken
Scatters in the night…now see
Moon-lighted mountains!

-Basho


Seek on high bare trails
Sky-reflecting violets…
Mountain-top jewels

-Basho


Mountain-rose petals
Falling, falling, falling now
Waterfall music

-Basho


April's air stirs in
Willow-leaves…a butterfly
Floats and balances.

-Basho

289

# Rhyme Scheme: Haiku

Dim the gray cow comes

Mooing mooing and mooing . . .

Out of the Morning mist.

-Issa

Arise from sleep, Cat,

and with great yawns and stretchings…

Amble out for love

-Issa

A gate made of twigs

With woven grass for hinges . . .

For a lock . . . this snail.

-Issa

# Rhyme Scheme: Haiku

Bits of song—what else?

I, a rider of the stream,

Lone between the clouds.

-Naguchi

But the march to life—

Break song to sing the new song!

Clouds leap, flowers bloom.

-Naguchi

Song of sea in rain,

Voice of the sky, earth and men!

List, song of my heart.

-Noguchi

On a withered twig,

Lo, the crow is sitting there,

Oh, this Autumn eve!

-Noguchi

# Rhyme Scheme: Simple 4-line

In this popular rhyme scheme,

only the second and fourth line rhyme.

**ABCB**

## Bug in a Jug by Unknown

| | |
|---|---|
| Curious fly, | A |
| Vinegar **jug**, | B |
| Slippery edge, | C |
| Pickled **bug**. | B |

## To Music by Oliver Herford

| | |
|---|---|
| Here's to Music, | A |
| Joy of **joys**! | B |
| One man's music's | C |
| Another man's **noise**. | B |

## Duties by Unknown

Think not of far-off duties,

But of duties which are **near**;

And, having once begun the work,

Resolve to **persevere**.

# Rhyme Scheme: Simple 4 Line

## Question by Unknown

Do you love me
Or do you not?
You told me once
But I forgot.

## The House in the Woods by Rachel Field

Deep in the old pine woods
Where moss like a rug is spread,
Stands a house with crumbling walls
And a roof of rusty red.

Grass sprouts in every chink;
The eaves are filmed with green.
If I crossed the threshold worn,
I should nevermore be seen.

For who but a witch would live
Where woods press tree on tree?
So I scurry by that place
Lest a spell be laid on me.

293

# Rhyme Scheme: Simple 4 Line

## Table Manners by Gelett Burgess

The Goops they lick their fingers,
And the Goops they lick their knives;
They spill their broth on the tablecloth—
Oh, they lead disgusting lives!

The Goops they talk while eating,
And loud and fast they chew;
And that is why I'm glad that I
Am not a Goop—are you?

## The Somethings by Ruth McEnery Stuart & Albert Bigelow Paine

A Something met a Something
In the mists of Shadowland.
They ran against each other,
And came quickly to a stand.

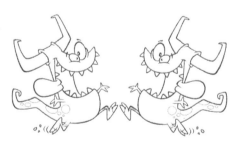

"And who are you?" said Something One.
And Something Two, said he,
"That's just the very question that
At once occurred to me."

# Rhyme Scheme: Simple 4 Line

## The Fisherman by Abbie Farwell Brown

The fisherman goes out at dawn
When every one's abed,
And from the bottom of the sea
Draws up his daily bread.

His life is strange; half on the shore
And half upon the sea—
Not quite a fish, and yet not quite
The same as you and me.

## Fishing by Vivan G. Gouled

I'm wearing old clothes,
My favorite kind.
They're faded and tattered,
But fish never mind.

My line's in the water
With squirming live bait.
I like to go fishing,
And dream while I wait.

# Rhyme Scheme: Simple 4 Line

## Forty Little Polliwogs by Unknown

Forty little polliwogs

Swimming in a ditch,

Each so near alike,

They don't know which is which.


Round and shiny bodies,

Wiggly, waggly tails,

Just like little fishes

All except their scales!

## Jumping and Tumbling by Unknown

In jumping and tumbling

We spend the whole day,

Till night by arriving

Has finished our play.


What then? One and all,

There's no more to be said,

As we tumbled all day,

So we tumble to bed.

# Rhyme Scheme: Simple 4 Line

## How Creatures Move by Unknown

The lion walks on padded paws,

The squirrel leaps from limb to limb,

While flies can crawl straight up a wall,

And seals can dive and swim.


The worm he wiggles all around,

The monkey swings by his tail,

And birds may hop upon the ground

Or spread their wings and sail.


But boys and girls

Have much more fun:

They leap and dance

And walk and run.

## Monster Problems by Lorrie L. Birchall

It's hard to be a monster;

I feel so out of place.

The people never understand—

this IS my happy face.

# Rhyme Scheme: Simple 4 Line

## My Goldfish by Dorothy Aldis

My darling little goldfish
Hasn't any toes;
He swims around without a sound
And bumps his hungry nose.

He can't get out to play with me,
Nor I get in to him,
Although I say: "Come out and play,"
And he—"Come in and swim."

## Mouths by Dorothy Aldis

I wish I had two little mouths
Like my two hands and feet—
A little mouth to talk with
And one that just could eat.

Because it seems to me mouths have
So many things to do—
All the time they want to talk
They are supposed to chew!

# Rhyme Scheme: Simple 4 Line

## In the Heart of a Seed by Kate L. Brown

In the heart of a seed,
Buried deep, so deep,
A dear little plant
Lay fast asleep!

"Wake!" said the sunshine,
"And creep to the light!"
"Wake!" said the voice
Of the raindrop bright.

The little plant heard
And it rose to see
What the wonderful
Outside world might be.

## Her Smile by Dorothy Aldis

It is so curly on her mouth
I love to see it there;
It comes from I don't quite know what,
It goes I don't know where . . .

# Rhyme Scheme: Limerick

A limerick is a silly five line poem with three long lines and two short lines.
Limericks often use creative (poetic) license by using
near rhymes, puns, made-up words or unusual spelling.
It follows the rhyme scheme: **AABBA**

## I Raised a Great Hullabaloo by Unknown

| | |
|---|---|
| I raised a great **hullabaloo** | **A** |
| When I found a large mouse in my **stew,** | **A** |
| Said the waiter, "Don't <u>shout</u> | **B** |
| And wave it <u>about,</u> | **B** |
| Or the rest will be wanting one, **too!**" | **A** |

## The Ocean by Unknown

I sat by the side of the ocean,

Tormenting myself with this nocean,

If a ship isn't taut,

Can she sail as she aut,

With the wind and the waves and commocean?

# Rhyme Scheme: Limerick

## The Old Man of the Hague by Edward Lear

There was an Old Man of the Hague,

Whose ideas were excessively vague;

    He built a balloon,

    To examine the moon,

That deluded Old Man of the Hague.

## The Old Man in the Tree by Edward Lear

There was an old man in a tree,

Whose whiskers were lovely to see;

    But the birds of the air,

    Plucked them perfectly bare,

To make themselves nests in that tree.

## The Old Man with a Beard by Edward Lear

There was an old man with a beard,

Who said, "It is just as I feared!—

    Two owls and a hen,

    Four Larks and a Wren,

Have all built their nests in my beard!"

# Rhyme Scheme: Limerick

## The Old Man of Peru by Edward Lear

There was an old man of Peru,

Who dreamed he was eating his shoe.

    He awoke in the night,

    In a terrible fright,

And found it was perfectly true.

## Another Old Man of Peru by Edward Lear

There was an old man of Peru,

Who watched his wife making a stew;

    But once, by mistake,

    In a stove she did bake,

That unfortunate man of Peru.

## There was a Young Boy in Quebec by Rudyard Kipling

There was a young boy in Quebec,

Who was buried in snow to his neck;

    When they said, "Are you friz?"

    He replied, "Yes, I is—

But we don't call this cold in Quebec."

# Rhyme Scheme: Limerick

## Ridiculous Mollusks
by Ruth McEnery Stuart & Albert Bigelow Paine

Ridiculous mollusks are we,

And dwell in the depths of the sea.

    Our bodies are jelly,

    And we haven't a belly

In the place where our bellies should be.

## Beauty by Richard Burton

For beauty I am not a star,

There are others more handsome by far,

    But my face—I don't mind it,

    For I am behind it;

It's the people in front that I jar.

## A Woodchuck by Unknown

A woodchuck would chuck him some wood—

He'd chuck all the wood that he could;

    The question arose,

    "How much you suppose,

A woodchuck would chuck if he could?"

# Rhyme Scheme: Limerick

## Genius by Edwin C. Ranck

There was once a young man quite erratic

Who lived all alone in an attic,

He wrote magazine verse

That made editors curse,

But his friends thought it fine and dramatic.

## There Once Were Three Owls by Unknown

There once were three owls in a wood

Who sang hymnals whenever they could;

What the words were about

One could never make out,

But one felt it was doing them good.

## The Athlete by Unknown

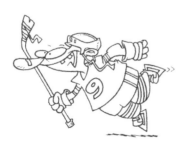

An athlete who lived in Milwaukee,

Attempted one day to play haukee,

But in less than a trice,

His feet left the ice,

In a manner exceedingly gaukee.

# Rhyme Scheme: Limerick

## A Young Lady of Lynn by Unknown

There was a young lady of Lynn,

Who was so uncommonly thin

    That when she essayed

    To drink lemonade,

She slipped through the straw and fell in.

## A Young Farmer of Leeds by Unknown

There was a young farmer of Leeds,

Who swallowed six packets of seeds,

    It soon came to pass,

    He was covered with grass,

And he couldn't sit down for the weeds.

## The 'Skeeter and Peter by Marie Bruckman MacDonald

There was a bright fellow named Peter,

Who struck at an active moskeeter,

    But the 'skeeter struck first

    And slackened his thirst,

For the 'skeeter was fleeter than Peter.

# Rhyme Scheme:  Limerick

## The Smiling Shark by Carolyn Wells

There was an old shark with a smile

So broad you could see it a mile.

    He said to his friends,

    As he sewed up the ends,

"It was really too wide for the style."

## The Armadillo by Carolyn Wells

There once was an arch Armadillo

Who built him a hut 'neath a willow;

    He hadn't a bed

    So he rested his head

On a young Porcupine for a pillow.

## The Man in the Moon -Traditional Nursery Rhyme

The Man in the Moon came tumbling down,

And asked the way to Norwich;

    He went by the south,

    And burnt his mouth,

With eating cold pease porridge.

# Rhyme Scheme: Limerick

## I'd Rather by Gelett Burgess

I'd rather have fingers than toes,
I'd rather have ears than a nose,
    And as for my hair,
    I'm glad it's all there,
I'll be awfully sad when it goes.

## A Young Man Named O'Neill by Unknown

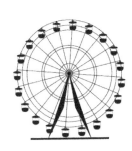

There was a young man named O'Neill,
Who went up a great Ferris wheel;
    But when half way 'round,
    He looked at the ground,
It cost him his ten dollar meal.

## The Ichthyosaurus (Ick-thee-oh-sor-us) by Unknown

There once was an Ichthyosaurus,
Who lived when the earth was all porous,
    But he fainted with shame,
    When he first heard his name,
And departed a long time before us.

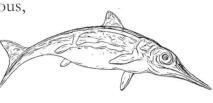

# Rhyme Scheme: Limerick

## The Grandfather Goat by Abbie Farwell Brown

There once was a grandfather goat,
Who thought he was able to vote;
   How did he behave him?
   The ballot they gave him
Soon vanished inside of his throat.

## The Dachshund by Wallace Rice

The Dachshund seems not to belong—
Born under a bureau, all wrong,
   You'll see him go by,
   Just a half a dog high,
And a dog and a half or so long.

## The Tiger by Unknown

There was a young lady of Niger
Who smiled as she rode on a tiger.
   They returned from the ride
   With the lady inside—
And the smile on the face of the tiger.

# Rhyme Scheme: Limerick

## Miss Dowd and the Mouse by Unknown

A mouse in her room woke Miss Dowd.

She was frightened and screamed very loud.

    Then a happy thought hit her—

    To scare off the critter,

She sat up in bed and meowed!

## A Girl and Three Bears by Lorrie L. Birchall

There once was a girl without cares,

who broke-in the home of three bears.

    Her trouble was deep,

    When she fell asleep,

And woke-up to furious stares.

## Flat Stanley by Lorrie L. Birchall

There once was a boy very flat,

So thin he was just like a mat.

    They mailed him around,

    By the air and the ground,

So he never knew where he was at.

# Rhyme Scheme: Limerick

## Mrs. Isosceles Tri by Clinton Brooks Burgess

Said Mrs. Isosceles Tri,

"That I'm sharp I've no wish to deny;

    But I do not dare

    To be perfectly square—

I'm sure if I did I should die!

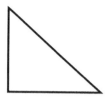

## Mr. Rectangular Square by Clinton Brooks Burgess

Said Mr. Rectangular Square,

"To say that I'm lost is unfair,

    For though you have found,

    That I never am round,

You knew all the time I was there."

## An Old Cat Named MacDuff by J.G. Francis

There was an old cat named MacDuff,

Who could joke till you cried, "That's enough!"

    His wife and his child,

    So persistently smiled,

That their cheeks had a permanent puff.

# Rhyme Scheme: Limerick

## Afternoon Tea by Gelett Burgess

There's nothing in Afternoon Tea,
To appeal to a person like me;
   There is little to eat,
   What there is is too sweet!
And I feel like a cow in a tree!

## A Young Lady Named Perkins by Unknown

There was a young lady named Perkins,
Who had a great fondness for gherkins;
   She went to a tea,
   And ate twenty-three,
Which pickled her internal workin's.

## A Young Fellow Named Paul by Unknown

There was a young fellow named Paul,
Who went to a fancy dress ball;
   They say, just for fun,
   He dressed as a bun,
And was eaten by dogs in the hall.

# Rhyme Scheme: Limerick

## A Young Fellow Named Beebee by Unknown

A certain young fellow named Beebee,

Wished to wed a young lady named Phoebe,

"But," he said, "I must see,

What the fee is to be,

before Phoebe can be Phoebe Beebee."

## The Lady of Kalamazoo by William Bellamy

There's a lady in Kalamazoo,

Who bites all her oysters in two;

She has a misgiving,

Should any be living,

They'd raise such a hullaballoo.

## A Young Person Called Kate by Mary Mapes Dodge

There was a young person called Kate,

Who sat on the stairs very late.

When asked how she fared,

She said she was scared,

But was otherwise doing first rate.

# What is Rhythm?

Certain words and syllables are emphasized over others,

making the internal "beat" or rhythm of a poem.

Some poems have a very regular rhythm,

while others have an irregular rhythm.


You can clap (or hum) the unique beat (or rhythm) of each poem.


## Little Things by Ebenezer Cobham Brewster

**Lit**tle drops of **wa**ter,        DUM di di di DUM di,

   **Lit**tle grains of **sand**,      DUM di di di DUM,

**Make** the mighty **o**cean      DUM di di di DUM di

   **And** the pleasant **land**.     DUM di di di DUM


**Thus** the little **min**utes,     DUM di di di DUM di,

   **Hum**ble though they **be**,    DUM di di di DUM,

**Make** the mighty **a**ges      DUM di di di DUM di

   **Of** e**ter**nity.         DUM di DUM di di.

# Rhythm

## The Little Elf by John Kendrick Bangs

I met a little Elf-man once,

Down where the lilies blow.

I asked him why he was so small,

And why he didn't grow.

He slightly frowned, and with his eye

He looked me through and through—

"I'm just as big for me," said he,

"As you are big for you."

## Little Fishes by Lorrie L. Birchall

Little fishes in the sea,

never can be too carefree.

Out there waiting in the dark,

is a very hungry shark!

## Design by Arthur Guiterman

The curving shore was made to hold the sea,

The hollyhock to hold the drowsy bee,

The columbine to hold a drop of dew,

And my two arms were fashioned just for you.

# Rhythm

## The Wave by John Drinkwater

Who says I'm not brave?

I let a wave

taller than two or three

people like me,

come rolling, rolling, rolling

out of the sea,

with bunches of spray,

in a most tremendous way,

all over me.

## Little by Dorothy Aldis

I am the sister of him

And he is my brother.

He is too little for us

To talk to each other.

So every morning I show him

My doll and my book;

But every morning he still is

Too little to look.

# Rhythm

## My Heart by Elizabeth Madox Roberts

My heart is beating up and down,

Is walking like some heavy feet.

My heart is going every day,

And I can hear it jump and beat.


At night before I go to sleep,

I feel it beating in my head;

I hear it jumping in my neck

And in the pillow on my bed.


And then I make some little words

To go along and say with it--

The men are sailing home from Troy,

And all the lamps are lit.

The men are sailing home from Troy,

And all the lamps are lit.

# Rhythm

## The Shoe Factory (Song of the Knot-Tyer) by Ruth Harwood

They told me
>    When I came
That this would be drudgery,
>    Always the same
Thing over and over
>    Day after day—
The same swift movement
>    In the same small way.


*Pick up,*
>    *Place,*
>>    *Push,*
>>>    *And it's tied.*

*Take off,*
>    *Cut,*
>>    *And put*
>>>    *It aside.*


Over and over
>    In rhythmical beat—
Some say it's drudgery
>    But to me it is sweet.

# Rhythm

## Caterpillar by Christina Georgina Rossetti

Brown and furry

Caterpillar in a hurry,

Take your walk

To the shady leaf, or stalk,

Or what not,

Which may be the chosen spot.

No toad spy you,

Hovering bird of prey pass by you;

Spin and die,

To live-again a butterfly.

## I'm Nobody! Who Are You? by Emily Dickinson

I'm nobody! Who are you?

Are you nobody, too?

Then there's a pair of us—don't tell!

They'd banish us, you know.


How dreary to be somebody!

How public, like a frog,

To tell your name the livelong day

To an admiring bog!

# Rhythm

## Playground by Ethel Romig Fuller

In the middle of town
There is a stray
Square of ground
Where children play.

Where little running
Feet have trod
Out every flower
And spear of sod.

And yet I think
It's gladder—lots—
Than any tended
Garden spots.

# What is a Simile?

A simile compares two unlike things using the words *like* or *as*.
Writers like to use similes because they are descriptive
and help create vivid pictures in a reader's head.

Example:

This stale piece of *bread* is <u>like a *rock*</u>.

## The Moon by Oliver Herford

**The Moon is like a big round cheese**
That shines above the garden trees,
And like a cheese grows less each night,
As though someone had had a bite.

## Easter by Joyce Kilmer

The **air is like a butterfly**
With frail blue wings.
The happy earth looks at the sky
And sings.

## The Scorpion by Hilaire Belloc

The **scorpion is as black as soot**,
He dearly loves to bite;
He is a most unpleasant brute
To find in bed at night.

320

# Simile

## Dandelion Down by Edith King

The silken dandelion down
sails off like a balloon,
I wish that I could ride on it
this breezy afternoon.

For it will glide by hedge and brook
where I can never stray,
and then will anchor soft as dreams
in meadows far away.

## The Night Will Never Stay by Eleanor Farjeon

The night will never stay,
The night will still go by,
Though with a million stars
You pin it to the sky,
Though you bind it with the blowing wind
And buckle it with the moon,
The night will slip away
Like sorrow or a tune.

# Simile

## The Jellyfish by Lorrie L. Birchall

The jellyfish—
A brainless fella,
looks just like
a big umbrella.

## When It's Hail by Lorrie L. Birchall

I love the whisper drops of rain
that plink upon my head,
but when it's hail, it feels to me
like pelting rocks instead.

## The Autumn Trees by Lorrie L. Birchall

The autumn trees are creepy,
when leaves have blown away.
The gnarled branches stretch their limbs,
like fingers old and gray.

# Simile

## Some People by Rachel Field

Isn't it strange some people make
you feel so tired inside,
your thoughts begin to shrivel up
like leaves all brown and dried!

But when you're with some other ones,
it's stranger still to find
your thoughts are thick as fireflies
all shiny in your mind!

## Oh, Look at the Moon by Eliza Lee Follen

Oh! Look at the moon,
How it's shining up there;
And see how it looks
Like a lamp in the air.

Last week it was smaller,
And shaped like a bow;
But now it's grown bigger,
And round as an O.

# Simile

## Queen Nefertiti by Unknown

Spin a coin, spin a coin,
All fall down;
Queen Nefertiti
stalks through the town.

Over the pavements
her feet go clack,
Her legs are as tall
as a chimney stack.

Spin a coin, spin a coin,
All fall down;
Queen Nefertiti
stalks through the town.

Her fingers flick
like snakes in the air,
The walls open wide
at her green-eyed stare.

Spin a coin, spin a coin,

All fall down;

Queen Nefertiti

stalks through the town.


Her voice is thin,

as the ghost of the bees;

She'll crumble your bones,

 she will make your blood freeze.


Spin a coin, spin a coin,

All fall down;

Queen Nefertiti

stalks through the town.


## Broomstick Time by Rowena Bastin Bennett

On Halloween, the witches fly

Like withered leaves across the sky,

Each with a broomstick for a steed

That gallops at tremendous speed.

Although I don't approve of witches

Who wear tall hats and live in ditches,

Still I am glad there is a day

When broomsticks have a chance to play.

# Simile

## Flint by Christina Georgina Rossetti

An emerald is as green as grass,
    A ruby red as blood;
A sapphire shines as blue as heaven;
    A flint lies in the mud.

A diamond is a brilliant stone,
    To catch the world's desire;
An opal holds a fiery spark;
    But a flint holds fire.

## A Warrior to His Horse –Lone Man, Sioux

My horse be swift in flight
Even like a bird;
My horse be swift in flight,
Bear me now in safety
Far from the enemy's arrows,
And you shall be rewarded
With streamers and ribbons red.

# Simile

## The Fly by Walter de la Mare

How large unto the tiny fly
  Must little things appear!—
A rosebud like a feather bed,
  Its prickle like a spear;
A dewdrop like a looking-glass,
  A hair like golden wire;
The smallest grain of mustard-seed
  As fierce as coals of fire;
A loaf of bread, a lofty hill;
  A wasp, a cruel leopard;
And specks of salt as bright to see
  As lambkins to a shepherd.

## The Sky by Abbie Farwell Brown

How good to lie a little while
And look up through the tree!
The sky is like a kind big smile
Bent sweetly over me.

# Simile

## Goldfish by Hilda Conkling

Like a shot of gold

Or an arrow darting

With thin gold wings

He swims . . .

Now around . . . then straight . . .

Then a swish of tail . . .

Then zigzag all along

With a kind of stiff smile . . .

In ponds or bowls

He swims and stares

Out of big popping eyes

Of ebony . . .

## The Mole by Edith King

The burrowing mole lives under the ground

Day in and day out, all the seasons year round;

Like a train in a tunnel, in darkness he goes,

And makes his own track with his feet and his nose.

# Simile

## The Storm by Edward Shanks

The rain slackens, the wind blows gently,
The gust grows gentle and stills,
And the thunder, like a breaking stick,
Stumbles about the hills.

## Rain in the City by Rachel Field

All the streets are a-shine with rain
The other side of my window pane.
Each motor car unrolls a track
of red or green on the asphalt's black.
Beneath umbrellas people ply
like giant toadstools stalking by.

## Archery by John B. Tabb

A bow across the sky
another in the river,
whence swallows upward fly,
like arrows from a quiver.

# Simile

## Jacky Frost by Laura E. Richards

Jacky Frost, Jacky Frost,

Crept around the house,

Sly as a silver fox,

Still as a mouse.

Out little Jenny came,

Blushing like a rose;

Up jumped Jacky Frost,

And pinched her little nose!

## From a Railway Carriage by Robert Louis Stevenson

Faster than fairies, faster than witches,

Bridges and houses, hedges and ditches;

And charging along like troops in a battle,

All through the meadows the horses and cattle:

All of the sights of the hill and the plain

Fly as thick as driving rain;

And ever again, in the wink of an eye,

Painted stations whistle by.

# What are Stanzas & Lines?

A **stanza** is like a poem's paragraph.

It's made up of **lines**.

Sometimes a stanza is called a **verse**.

Stanzas have different names based on their number of lines:

2 lines = couplet

3 lines = tercet

4 lines = quatrain

5 lines = cinquain

## My Wife Peggy by Anne L. Huber

Stanza #1 has four lines

My little wife Peggy

Loves apples and pears;

Her left leg fell down

And broke all our stairs.

Stanza #2 has four lines

Oh, no, that is not it.

It was my wife Peg,

Who fell down the stairs

And broke her left leg.

# Stanzas & Lines

## The Secret by Unknown

We have a secret, just we three,

The robin, and I, and the sweet cherry-tree;

The bird told the tree, and the tree told me,

And nobody knows it but just us three.


But of course the robin knows it best,

Because she built the—I shan't tell the rest;

And laid the four little—something in it—

I'm afraid I shall tell it every minute.


But if the tree and the robin don't peep,

I'll try my best the secret to keep;

Though I know when the little birds fly about

Then the whole secret will be out.


How many **stanzas** are there?

How many **lines** are there?

Are the stanzas organized as a **couplet**, **tercet**, **quatrain**, or **tercet**?

# Stanzas & Lines

Some stanzas can have many lines.

Some verse paragraphs might be larger, some smaller.

And free verse poems do not follow a formal poem structure.

## Rainy Nights by Rachel Field

Always on rainy nights
When my candle is blown out
And I am all alone,
I hear strange footsteps fall
Out in the dark and wet—
Footsteps that only come
With the rain, and go with it—
Noisily swashing by
Like the boots of buccaneers,
Or the tread of old sea captains
Tramping on salty decks
Of ships with figureheads,
So old the sea has forgotten
Their names and the ports they sailed from.
Sometimes in soft spring rains
The steps are light and hurried,
Pattering by like children
With little scuffling sounds,
Up and down in the dark
Long corridors of night.
Whose footsteps are they, and why
Do they come and go like that,
And what do they want in the rain?

# What is Syntax?

Syntax is the **order of words** used in

a sentence, a line of verse, or dialogue.

Poets like to play with language,

so they sometimes put words in an unexpected order

for creative effect.

Examples of poetry lines that play with syntax (word order):

*When I was just a Kitten small*

"The Puncture" by Oliver Herford

*I'll try my best the secret to keep*

"The Secret" by Unknown

*Like a river down the gutter roars*

"Rain in Summer" by Henry W. Longfellow

*The wizard of the woods is he*

"The Woodpecker" by John B. Tabb

*Everyone for me does run*

"Gold" by Laura E. Richards

*She found herself within a parlor charming*

"Goldilocks and the Three Bears" by Walter Crane

# Syntax

## A Centipede by Unknown

A centipede was happy quite

Until a frog in fun

Said, "Pray, which leg comes after which?"

This raised her mind to such a pitch,

She lay distracted in the ditch,

Considering how to run.

## March by Unknown

"Oh, March, why are you scolding?

    Why not more cheerful be?"

"Because," said growling, blustering March,

    "The whole world scolds at me."

## One Misty, Moisty Morning by Unknown

One misty, moisty morning,

When cloudy was the weather,

I chanced to meet an old man,

Clothed all in leather.

He began to compliment

And I began to grin.

How do you do? And how do you do?

And how do you again?

335

# Syntax

## Old Man Schooner by Rachel Field

Old Man Schooner, where have you been?

    Where will you go from here?

What harbors strange have you anchored in?

    To what far port do you steer?

Was your topsail patched in Zanzibar?

    Your cargo stowed in Spain?

Did the spray of the four seas spray your decks

    In a stinging, salty rain?

# Which Poetry Devices?

Poems often have **more than one** poetry device.

Can you recognize the poetry devices in these poems?

(For help: See The Poetry Device Checklist on pgs. 345-346)

## Glimpse in Autumn by Jean Starr Untermeyer

Ladies at the ball
    Are not so fine as these
    Richly brocaded trees
That decorate the fall.

They stand against a wall
    Of crisp October sky,
    Their plumed heads held high,
Like ladies at the ball.

## A Fire by Rachel Field

Why does a fire eat big sticks of wood?
I shouldn't like to have that for my food.
But the flames all lick their lips—it must be good!

# Which Poetry Devices?

## The Dirigible by Ralph Bergengren

The only real airship
That I've ever seen
Looked more like a fish
Than a flying machine.

It made me feel funny,
And just as if we
Were all of us down
On the floor of the sea.

A big whale above us
Was taking a swim,
And we little fishes
Were staring at him.

## Moonbeam by Hilda Conkling

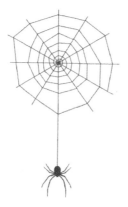

Moonbeam steps down the
Silken ladder
Woven by Mrs. Spider
To ask her to spin him a net
To catch the stars.

# Which Poetry Devices?

## A Wasted Day by Frances Cornford

I spoiled the day;
    Hotly, in haste.
All the calm hours
    I gashed and defaced.

Let me forget,
    Let me embark
Sleep for my boat
    And sail through the dark.

Till a new day
    Heaven shall send,
Whole as an apple,
    Kind as a friend.

## The Storm by Dorothy Aldis

In my bed all safe and warm
I like to listen to the storm.
The thunder rumbles loud and grand—
The rain goes splash and whisper; and
The lightning is so sharp and bright
It sticks its fingers through the night.

339

# Which Poetry Devices?

## The Sandpiper by Celia Thaxter

Across the lonely beach we flit,

One little sandpiper and I,

And fast I gather, bit by bit,

The scattered driftwood, bleached and dry.

The wild waves reach their hands for it,

The wild wind raves, the tide runs high,

As up and down the beach we flit,

One little sandpiper and I.

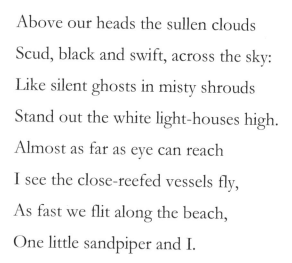

Above our heads the sullen clouds

Scud, black and swift, across the sky:

Like silent ghosts in misty shrouds

Stand out the white light-houses high.

Almost as far as eye can reach

I see the close-reefed vessels fly,

As fast we flit along the beach,

One little sandpiper and I.

## Last Dance by Harriet King

The soft wind and the yellow leaves

Are having their last dance together.

# Which Poetry Devices?

## Little Papoose by Charles Myall

Rock-a-bye, hush-a-bye, little papoose,

The stars come into the sky;

The whippoorwill's crying, the daylight is dying,

The river runs murmuring by.

The pine trees are slumbering, little papoose,

The squirrel has gone to his nest;

The robins are sleeping,

the mother bird's keeping

The little ones warm at her breast.

The roebuck is dreaming, my little papoose,

His mate lies asleep at his side;

The breezes are pining, the moonbeams are shining

All over the prairie wide.

Then hush-a-bye, rock-a-bye, little papoose,

You sail on the river of Dreams;

Dear Manitou loves you and watches above you

Till time when the morning light gleams.

# Which Poetry Devices?

## The Caterpillar by Robert Graves

Under this loop of honeysuckle,

A creeping, colored caterpillar,

I gnaw the fresh green hawthorn spray,

I nibble it leaf by leaf away.

Down beneath grow dandelions,

Daisies, old-man's-looking-glasses;

Rooks flap croaking across the lane.

I eat and swallow and eat again.


Here come raindrops helter-skelter;

I munch and nibble unregarding:

Hawthorn leaves are juicy and firm

I'll mind my business: I'm a good worm.


When I'm old, tired, melancholy,

I'll build a leaf-green mausoleum

Close by, here on this lovely spray,

And die and dream the ages away.

Some say worms win resurrection,

With white wings beating flitter-flutter,

But wings or a sound sleep, why should I care?

Either way I'll miss my share.


Under this loop of honeysuckle,

A hungry, hairy caterpillar,

I crawl on my high and swinging seat,

And eat, eat, eat—as one ought to eat.

# Which Poetry Devices?

## Memory Book by Althea Randolph

Our memory is like a book,

The pages written on

With things we've said, and things we've thought,

And deeds that we have done.


Now let this Book of Memory

Be sacred to us all,

Write nothing on a page of it,

We'd care not to recall.


Then when the leaves are backward turned,

To read the story told,

There'll be no word, or thought, or deed,

But of the purest gold.

# Which Poetry Devices?

## If I Knew the Box by Maud Wyman

If I knew the box where smiles were kept,

No matter how large the key

Or strong the bolt, I would try so hard

'Twould open, I know, for me.

Then over the land and sea broadcast

I'd scatter the smiles to play,

That the children's faces might hold them fast

For many and many a day.


If I knew a box that was large enough

To hold all the frowns I meet,

I would gather them, each and every one,

From nursery, school and street.

Then, folding and holding, I'd pack them in

And turn the monster key,

And hire a giant to drop the box

To the depths of the deep, deep sea,

# Which Poetry Devices?

(Here's an especially fun poem to explore poetry devices.)

## Free Verse by Robert Graves

I now delight

In spite

Of the might

And the right

Of classic tradition,

In writing

And reciting

Straight ahead,

Without let or omission,

Just any little rhyme

In any little time

That runs in my head;

Because, I've said,

My rhymes no longer shall stand arrayed

Like Prussian soldiers on parade

That march,

Stiff as starch,

Foot to foot,

Boot to boot,

Blade to blade,

Button to button

Cheeks and chops and chins like mutton.

No! No!

My rhymes must go

Turn 'ee, twist 'ee,

Twinkling, frosty,

Will-o'-the-wisp-like, misty;

Rhymes I will make

Like Keats and Blake

And Christina Rossetti,

With run and ripple and shake.

How pretty

To take

A merry little rhyme

In a jolly little time

And poke it,

And choke it,

Change it, arrange it,

Straight-lace it, deface it,

Pleat it with pleats,

Sheet it with sheets

Of empty conceits,

And chop and chew,

And hack and hew,

And weld it into a uniform stanza,

And evolve a neat,

Complacent, complete,

Academic extravaganza!

# The Poetry Device Checklist

Here's a checklist to help you identify poetry devices
in some of the poems you read.

Title of Poem: _____

Poet: _____

- ☐ Alliteration example(s)?_____

  _____

- ☐ Allusion to what? _____

- ☐ Anaphora example(s)? _____

- ☐ Anthropomorphism example(s)?_____

  _____

- ☐ Assonance example(s)?_____

  _____

- ☐ Consonance example(s)? _____

  _____

- ☐ Creative/Poetic License example(s)?_____

  _____

- ☐ Eye Rhyme example(s)? _____

- ☐ Fable poem?_____

- ☐ Hyperbole example(s)? _____

  _____

- ☐ Imagery example(s)? _____

  _____

- ☐ Inference: What can you infer?_____

  _____

- ☐ Internal Rhyme example(s)? _____

  _____

- ☐ Metaphor example(s)?_____

  _____

- ☐ Meter: Is it regular or irregular? _____

- ☐ Mood & Tone: How would you describe them? _____

☐ Narrative Poem?

☐ Onomatopoeia example(s)?_____

_____

☐ Parody: What's being parodied? _____

☐ Personification example(s)?_____

_____

☐ Point of View:

    o  1st Person (I, We)

    o  2nd Person (You)

    o  3rd (He, She, They)

    o  More than one Point of View

☐ Pun example(s)? _____

_____

☐ Refrain example(s)?_____

_____

☐ Repetition: What's repeated?_____

☐ Rhyme Scheme:

    o  Free Verse? (no rhyme scheme)

    o  Monorhyme? (AAAA)

    o  Alternate Rhyme? (ABAB)

    o  Couplet? (AA, BB, CC, …)

    o  Tercet? (AAA, ABA, ABC)

    o  Haiku?(ABC)

    o  Simple 4 Line? (ABCB)

    o  Limerick? (AABBA)

    o  Other rhyme scheme _____

☐ Simile example(s)? _____

_____

☐ Stanzas & lines: How many of each?_____

☐ Syntax: Unusual word order example(s)?_____

_____

More Notes: _____

_____

# Title Index

# First Lines Index

# Author Index

Made in the USA
Middletown, DE
08 March 2022